FOOTBALL AFTER PEP

THE EVOLUTION OF THE GAME SINCE THE ARRIVAL OF GUARDIOLA ON THE BENCH

ALBERT MORÉN

Football after Pep / Albert Morén - 1st ed. - LIBROFUTBOL.com, 2021.

232 pages; 15,2 x 22,9 cm.

ISBN 978-987-8370-80-4

1. Football. 2. Football Clubs. 3. Anecdotes. I. Title.
CDD 796.33409

FOOTBALL AFTER PEP
by Albert Morén

Cover design: Luciano Medvetkin Translation: Daniel Campos	Photo of author: © Albert Morén
© 2021– Albert Morén © 2021– LIBROFUTBOL.com	All rights reserved

ISBN 978-987-8370-80-4 — 1st edition: January 2021

ediciones@librofutbol.com

+54 9 11 2215 1982

librofutbol

Olga Cossettini 1112 - oficina 8F - Ciudad de Buenos Aires - Argentina

To Dani.

ÍNDICE

INTRODUCTION

GUARDIOLA, FROM A NAME TO AN ADJECTIVE

Is it possible to hear the same again after listening to one of the best compositions by Johann Sebastian Bach? Does silence mean the same when nostalgia kicks in with brilliant musical notes? Is it possible to keep watching and understanding the world in the same manner when we have watched it from an unknown place?[1]

The greatest talents in a given art or discipline are not so simply because of conquering limits in their given field, but to also add new layers of meaning. To go further than their own margins. To extend the universe from the known, discovering worlds until then undisclosed and educating perceptions of others from the creation of a reality unimagined beforehand. To point out and indicate where perceptions were not previously seen.

This is how it has also occurred throughout the history of football, with protagonists as individuals and joint collectives who have pushed their knowledge beyond their borders. They have provoked and shaken concepts already used, suddenly, as a cause of their legacy and footprint, extended by their rationality. The manner of understand-

---

1 Portabella, Pere (2007). *Die stille vor Bach* [*The silence before Bach*]. Films 59.

ing football and the expectations in place go hand-in-hand on purpose, change as a result of its legacy.

At the end of the 1990's, for example, *France Football* magazine wrote shortly after the AC Milan side led by Arrigo Sacchi that football or soccer will never be the same. It was a period of time where the "rossoneri" reign in Europe, thanks to a revolutionary football played that was imposed against their rivals, that captivated its successors and, also, contributed in modifying a regulation that it had succeeded in defeating. Their interpretation and application of the off-side tactic first found and later exploited a loophole that forced the game's governing body and law enforcers to rectify. AC Milan had reached new heights. It had overstepped limits.

Some years later, FC Barcelona went through a spell under the nicknamed *"Dream Team"*, a project born in 1988 with the arrival of Dutchman Johan Cruyff to the "blaugrana" bench. On the way to their fourth consecutive league title and the endorsement of a maiden 1991-92 European Cup trophy (prior to the naming UEFA Champions League), the unique philosophy of play by the manager had become the glass through which the game was distilled from the surface of the Camp Nou. A new path was forged to approach it. A new way of understanding the game. A filter set from seduction and victory, with which the personal and creative logic of the architect of that team was enthroned. An influence with the capacity to transform reality that Romário, the cartoon Brazilian striker[2], summed up with the eloquent phrase, "football is seen through Cruyff's eyes".

On the back of the news of the Dutch coach's death in 2016, Pep Guardiola, his most prominent pupil, recalled the maestro: "Cruyff was like that teacher you always

---

2 Besa, Ramón (2020). Romario would unmark himself walking. *Romário se desmarcaba caminando. El País newspaper.*

wanted to have class with, because he made you love it (...) he opened up a new world for me, a fascinating film"[3].

Guardiola's successes are the penultimate chapter in the story. An influence, captivating in victory and style, amplified by an era in which access to information is much more direct, immediate, and universal. A spokesperson without barriers thrown into the world of football as a contagion. As a legacy to follow, a challenge to adapt to, or simply a novel question to address. To interrogate football, whether its own and that of others, with a borrowed gaze.

In 2011, the Tate Modern in London and the Fundació Joan Miró in Barcelona jointly organised "Joan Miró. The Staircase of Evasion", an exhibition on the occasion of which a series of debates on the Catalan artist were also organised. In one of them, entitled "Miró after Miró", philosopher Xavier Antich addressed the question of the Miró myth, or, as he would describe it, the process by which Miró ceased to be a proper name and became an adjective. In a category. In an appellative used not to speak of Miró himself but, through him, to observe others. From Miró to Miróian. Antich wondered at the time whether, precisely, this exercise of obligatory synthesis, of creating a sketch based on some general features of the author, did not run the risk of concealing aspects of his oeuvre and his work that were less docile and malleable when it came to creating a mould, but equally consubstantial to his art. If, in order to create the adjective, it was necessary to be unfair and inaccurate with the proper name. If that part of Miró that inhabited others had ended up overshadowing the part of Miró that remained his alone. If Miró could be rescued from the prison of his own adjective.

The pages of this book propose a journey between the name Guardiola and the man himself and Guardiola as

---

3 López, Marcos (2016). Guardiola: "Johan's legacy is infinite, indestructible". *Guardiola: "El legado de Johan es infinito, indestructible". El Periódico de Catalunya.*

an adjective. Between a Guardiola in block capital letters and a Guardiolian in lower case letters. Between those who belong only to the manager and his work at FC Barcelona, Bayern Munich and Manchester City, and to the part belonging to his style of football play that already belongs to others. To chase an influence and importance of a manager at a given moment when redefining limits and meanings in specific determined aspects of play and the very nature of those who practice it. Guardiola is a driving force for change. A journey through a bridge that rises between the football played before Guardiola the native from Santpedor and the football employed after Pep. Just how much football is there in Guardiola beyond Pep?

CHAPTER 1

GOING OUT AS A COUPLE[4]

> "If you have the ball, the other player doesn't have it"[5]
>
> JOHAN CRUYFF

On the 20th of May 1992, Fútbol Club Barcelona conquered their maiden European Cup (prior to the naming of the Champions League) in their history, with Johan Cruyff on the bench and Pep Guardiola on the field. The Cup title settled a symbolic debt with the Catalan club because after losing the finals of 1961 in Bern and the 1986 edition in Seville, the European Cup had been converted into an almost traumatic obsession for the club and its surroundings. With its giant social mass, a history plagued with first class football players and star signings and with one of the most impressive football stadiums in the world, Barça had it all for the ages in a period where the great clubs of the continent were acknowledged, but the sport-

---

4 T itle under which, in June 2006, an article by Pep Guardiola was published in the newspaper El País about the Mexican national football team's ball control at the World Cup in Germany..

5 Aquest Any, Cent! (1999). Johan Cruyff. Televisió de Catalunya – CCMA.

ing prowess and achievements that the others had were elusive to them. Against this backdrop, the team's triumph by Cruyff at Wembley, together with his triumphant campaign in the domestic Spanish La Liga competition, meant a certain epiphany and stroke of good luck.

He fixed an imaginary "*culé*" collective path, a way to search for victory that enabled him to pick up wins that up until then were denied. Linking up and attaching a certain game model with his triumphs unlike beforehand under illustrious names related to the football ideas and proposals of Cruyff, like Rinus Michels, César Luis Menotti or Laureano Ruiz. The difference to them was, Cruyff educated his players from the point of view of defeat. Barça had never won so much in those years following the Dutchman's recipe , an event that consolidated a truth in the minds of fans. A magical formula, headed by their own past history, like a refuge in order to look back in search of answers. His unique way of approaching and learning side-by-side with success, and his disposition of service stems from the policy of incorporating coaches and players right through to the philosophy of junior grassroots football.

In that final, fixated into club history folklore at Barça courtesy of that winning free-kick scored by Ronald Koeman outside the 18-yard box, Pep Guardiola contributed playing 112 minutes and dictated the rhythm and tempo by distributing from midfield, a position very well known in the system in place by Cruyff, also known as the role of the number 4. In the football employed by the Dutch manager, the different movements away from the opposition marker whilst also indicating the location on the pitch that incorporated, as well, the roles that had to be fulfilled by the player in that given position. In saying this, for example, the 7, along with being a right winger or outside-right needs to be a patient player waiting and holding the ball along the flanks, fast, deep and daring to take on one-on-ones or 1v1 situations. Linking a particular number to a particular profile or role of a player, the manager linked up the where and how under a same banner and definition[6].

Despite Guardiola being the number 4 for Cruyff par excellence, the Santpedor native played in that memorable final played against Sampdoria with the number 10 on his back. In those years, whenever Ronald Koeman was in the starting line-up, the number 4 belonged to him, something that was very common for what many considered to be the most important player in the *Dream Team*.

Although at that time, squads still lined-up from numbers 1 to 11 without each number having an officially pre-assigned owner, numbers were often retained game to game, match after match for the most senior-aged players, and Ronald Koeman was one of them. One of his most iconic teammates, Jose Mari Bakero, summed up Koeman's ascendancy in Cruyff's Barça game as follows: "When Ronald played well, Barça played well. When he didn't play well, we still won, but we didn't play well. He was the most decisive player"[7].

The fact that Koeman wore the number 4 without occupying the place that in Cruyff's system was linked to this number hides one of the secrets of the formation of that memorable team. The coach's initial intentions were to make his fellow countryman the number 4 at Barça, a role he had already played under him at Ajax Amsterdam. It was not just any role, but in Johan's design it originally had a very important tactical function. In Cruyff's game plan, his team would attack with three forwards and four midfielders in a diamond formation in midfield, leaving it to the 4 to allow this attacking organisation to be compatible with a defensive line of four players when the team did not have the ball. Cruyff wanted to attack with three

---

6 Torquemada, Ricard (2011), *Fórmula Barça. A journey inside a team that has discovered eternity. Viatge a l'interior d'un equip que ha descobert l'eternitat.* Valls, España: Cossetània Edicions.

7 Peyret, Dídac (2020). Koeman, the anchor of the Dream Team. *Koeman, el ancla del Dream Team. Sport.*

fullbacks but defend with four. The 4 was, therefore, two players in one. A player who, like the Franz Beckenbauer who during the 1970s rivalled Cruyff for domination of European football, would play as a centre-back in defence and a midfielder in attack. It was not in vain that Johan often referred to this player as an "advanced sweeper or libero" or an "attacking defender".

Luis Milla, a Barça youth player and the first Barça player in whom Cruyff placed his trust to carry out the functions of the 4, underlines the hybrid nature of the position in the Dutch coach's approach: "Without the ball I played as a central midfielder although I didn't have the physique of a central midfielder, but then when we had the ball I would go into midfield (...) I felt at ease because in the reserve team we often used a 1-4-2-3-1 or a 1-4-4-4-2 and I was the more defensive midfielder. Guillermo Amor was the offensive midfielder. In this sense my role was similar. I was the midfielder who stayed in the position the most and the one who covered the back of the other midfielders in the reserve team (...) In my position it was important to keep shape and hold the position role, help the backline three, get in as a central holding midfielder when the opposition attacked down the flank because otherwise a defender would be missing, and to be close to the central midfielder at certain moments. It was a fundamental position"[8].

But Koeman, Cruyff's first 4 at Ajax, could not also be a 4 at Barça. His move to the Catalan side was delayed for a year, and when it finally happened, not only was Milla already surprisingly filling the position, but Ronald encountered some difficulties in getting to grips with a different kind of football. "Cruyff started the pre-season by putting me in my usual position, but he soon realised that in Spain, in my usual place in front of the defence and behind

---

8 En un momento dado (2021). Interview with Luis Milla. Extracted from: https://eumd.es/2021/04/entrevista-luis-milla/

the midfield, I will always have a man on top of me acting as a dribbler, so he tried to devise a new position for me"9.

The place Cruyff found for him was a few metres further down the pitch, as a centre-back, first behind Milla and then behind Guardiola, a solution that not only allowed Koeman to fit in, but also opened up new possibilities for both the coach and the team. His vision, his technique and, particularly, his almost infinite ability to move the ball both on the short pass and the long shot, gave Cruyff an infallible tool for building play from the back. The early stages of every play would be of exquisite quality, generating an early advantage that he was able to pass on, like a gift, to the other players in the team.

That is why, Guardiola himself recalls, Johan Cruyff "used to say that the most important players for a team to play well with the ball in possession are its defenders. If you play out well, you can build-up well; if you don't, there is no option"10.

In Cruyff's idea of the game, as later in Guardiola's, the desire to have control of the ball guided much of his behaviour. The Dutchman summed it up by stating that "if you want to attack, you have to dominate the game. And you can only dominate the game if you have the ball"11, and the man from Santpedor would fulfil it by saying that "I have always thought that what players really want is that they have the ball (...) It is something very akin to schoolyard football, very playful: I want the ball"12. Control of the ball is understood not as an objective in itself, but as a means more favourable so to conquer.

---

9 Morén, Albert (2017). *En un momento dado*: Defensa de ataque. Extracted from: https://eumd.es/2017/05/importancia-ronald-koeman-dream-team-johan-cruyff/

10 Guardiola, Josep (2006). *Salir de novios. El País newspaper.*

11 Aquest Any, Cent! (1999). Johan Cruyff. Televisió de Catalunya – CCMA.

12 LaTdT (2020). *Parlem de Futbol.* Let's talk about football. Corporació Catalana de Mitjans Audiovisuals.

In that desire to become the protagonist with possession of the ball, the capacity to construct attacking playing out clean from the back acquires a fundamental role. Firstly, because in increases the possibilities of your team to not lose the ball. This is how analyst and former player Àlex Delmàs defends the approach, when reviewing how "one comes out directly, your chances of continuing the sequence of play are lower. This brings you to the dependence of luck and randomness, onto a second ball into a lottery or raffle by hoofing the ball or by the opposing player clearing the ball entering your zone"[13].

Álvaro Benito, also a former footballer and coach, regarding this issue declares himself less categorical or adamant, by considering that "there are teams when they hoof the ball long, they know perfectly where the ball is directed, why it is directed and are very well prepared for what is coming. For them it is a given situation that is not a huge uncertainty. Another thing is to steal the ball from you because you are outnumbered and overwhelmed, but there are teams that what they look for is direct play and they do it very well" but adds that "what I do believe is that when you omit and eliminate a line of high pressure by way of a pass or by the conduction or dribbling of the ball, it gives you a lot of advantages. This is because from this starting point you have numerical superiority. You can assemble, you can join and attract, drag or draw-in your rivals... It may be very risky, but it rewards you very much"[14].

This comment by Álvaro introduces the second aspect that relates to the release of the ball coming out from the back with the possibility of teams having control and dominance of the ball: an opening build-up from the outset that is favourable that not only limits your chances of losing the ball, nevertheless, contributes to improving the

---

13 *En un momento dado* (2021). Interview with Àlex Delmàs. Extracted from: https://eumd.es/2021/04/entrevista-alex-delmas/

14 *En un momento dado* (2021). Interview with Álvaro Benito. Extracted from: https://eumd.es/2021/04/entrevista-alvaro-benito/

context in a decisive way of keeping the ball. Juanma Lillo, one of the biggest influences of Guardiola and who was formerly his manager in Mexico with Dorados de Sinaloa and later part of his technical staff at Manchester City, illustrates it all with the following: "Tell me how you release the ball, and I shall tell you how you will arrive, because if you do not play out clean enough from the back it will not be easy to end up with an advantage further up front"[15]. The play and release of the ball from the back should be understood as a concept of a run-up series of communicating vessels that accumulate advantages during its path sequence, it must lead the game along the way towards the opponent's goal in the most favourable of conditions possible.

In this regard, there are two episodes in the track record of Guardiola on the side-lines especially insightful. Firstly revealed by Thierry Henry on British broadcaster *Sky Sports* explaining how one of the initial football deals established at Barça between the coach and the players concluded that one of the key duties of a manager was to achieve, by way of the white board, that the ball may reach the feet of football players in the top attacking third in the best playing conditions possible, leaving them with the task of harnessing that gift to stamp a difference courtesy of their talent and individual quality[16]. The deal hid a second embedded pact, as it was that, in exchange of a manager conceding leeway to his players close to the opposition's goal, they had to beforehand commit and put themselves at the service of their plan in order to advance to it. The second episode is retold by Martí Perarnau in his book *Pep Guardiola. The metamorphosis*, bringing to light and unearthing a conversation between the Manchester

---

15 Mis entrenamientos de fútbol I (2018). The positional game. *Juego de posición*. Extracted from: **https://www.misentrenamientosdefutbol.com/diccionario/juego-de-posicion**

16 Teoría Táctica Fútbol (12th November, 2018). Henry about Guardiola's game. *Henry sobre el juego de Guardiola*. Extracted from: **https://www.youtube.com/watch?v=ly5La27wx90**

City head coach and brother Pere Guardiola, in which they question the real importance of playing the ball out from the back, as Pep responds by saying that "in our way of playing, coming out clean and crisp with the ball is the base to everything (...) It is not the same when the right winger receives the ball directly from the centre back as it is to receive the ball from the inside half. If receiving the ball from the central defender, it will almost always to be covered without any problem. On the other hand, if receiving the ball from the inside or central midfielder it will be much more difficult to cover and defend"[17].

One of the central ideas of playing out from the back with control of the ball, in the same way teams led by Pep Guardiola propose, is the search for the free player, the free man. Detecting the player in the best scenario to receive a pass at disposal and readiness or, in the case it does not occur, the activation of a series of mechanisms to pop-up and force its emergence. "If I am a central defender and a winger is approaching by pressing towards me, my full-back will be free: the ball must go to my lateral wing-back. If the pressing opposition player is the central forward, my other central defender is free: the ball must go to him. If the oncoming player applying pressure is the midfield playmaker, the centre half will be free thus the ball must go to him"[18]. The most prominent action in this given moment of play is the pass, given the fact that it is the technical gesture and execution that allows the ball to arrive to a teammate as quick as possible.

Nonetheless, the pass may also serve to free up the vigilance or supervision of an opponent in a future scenario for a player on the receiving end of the ball, by way of solutions like the third man. "When playing the ball, the concept of a third player is basic —argues Àlex Delmàs—,

---

17 Perarnau, Martí (2016), *Pep Guardiola. La metamorfosis.* Barcelona, España: Editorial Córner.

18 GOL (24th July, 2019). *90 minutos con Pep Guardiola.* Extracted from: https://youtu.be/hNCjnwKEea4

meaning the ball will not arrive to its final destination with a direct pass but rather through an intermediary or middleman. Normally this involves a player further away who can turn away facing a teammate". It is about a resource especially present featuring proposals and options of positional play the way Pep Guardiola employs and consists of a triangulation that may allow the ball to a player seen in first instance, through the implementation of an earlier pass to another player.

"Imagine Piqué *wanting to play with me*, but I am heavily marked, I am covered and unavailable – asked Xavi Hernández to Martí Perarnau in his book "Senda de campeones"–, well, it is clear that Piqué is unable to pass me the ball, so I move away and drag my marker with me. Here, therefore Messi drops and becomes the second man. Piqué is the 1st, Messi the 2nd and I am the 3rd. Piqué plays the ensuing ball to the 2nd man, Messi returns it, and this is where I show up at this point in time, baffling my defending marker left clueless, and Piqué will as a result, pass me the ball completely unmarked. If whoever is marking me is ball-watching, it is impossible to see me shift away into space, therefore I appear as a third-man option. We now create superiority"[19].

A second way for a free player to pop up has to do with the control and steering of the ball, a technical gesture or skill where the footballer moves the ball from one area of the pitch to another, not by way of a pass but by moving around with the ball. By doing so, by all means, when a teammate is free is in possession of the ball, whilst all teammates receive direct marking from an opponent. Control of the ball is, therefore, a resource aimed both at taking advantage of the freedom given to the player who has the ball and, focused mainly at generating to option of a pass by causing a break in one of the markers: the foot-

---

19 Perarnau, Martí (2011), *Senda de campeones. De La Masía al Camp Nou*. Barcelona, España: Salsa Books.

ball player with the ball will advance in the direction towards the opponent's goal, forcing the opponent to come out to defend and forcing to leave the paired marker free.

"When coming out with the ball there is a rule of thumb: the opponent pressing towards you, always leaves a free player", concludes Delmàs. "You must always look at who is coming towards you, because in that zone you will always have a teammate free (...) The control of the ball is for given situations where you do not have your opponent all over you and breathing behind your neck. When your opponent is waiting for you and you have to draw in an opponent so from that point you can find spaces between the lines. Whereas a pass needs to be executed when you have already identified the free player (...). There are moments where you must know when to interpret to play the ball to control and pass or when to hold and conduct the ball and draw or attract, suck-in your markers. This is something that Piqué does very well, he has been doing it his whole life and does it naturally".

Every scenario corresponds to an action. The ability of the player both to identify the context and to decide on the most appropriate solution will ultimately make the difference. It is not for nothing that Guardiola argues that "the problem is not playing out. The problem is to make the right decision depending on the opponent"[20]. "With Manchester City we made the record number of passes in a Champions League game against FC Basel. But 80% of the passes were between the centre-backs. That's no good," recalls Santpedor native. If your possession has no emotion, if it has no life, if it doesn't serve to generate danger, it makes no sense"[21].

---

20 LaTdT (2020). *Parlem de Futbol.* Let's talk about football. Corporació Catalana de Mitjans Audiovisuals.

21 GOL (24th July, 2019). *90 minutos con Pep Guardiola.* Extracted from: https://youtu.be/hNCjnwKEea4

Juanma Lillo points in the same direction when he states: "Do not play if you are not looking to generate anything. Play to overcome and break lines. Look for the third man and the second action of play (to create 1v1); and thus leave the farthest player. Generate superiority in the next line. Do not touch the ball wide if you do not provoke anything"[22].

Along with the pass and control of the ball, which are two actions of play that are more directly linked to the ball, the ball is directly linked when played out along the ground and finds a player in position which is the third way to generate numerical superiority and find a free man. This is how Johan Cruyff found the way to decide to move without a defender onto you because against two forwards it would be enough to play with a backline three to win in numbers, and also when playing out from the back, it is common to see teams prioritising this moment of play involving a player from your own team rather than your opponent in the first movement of pressure. "It is something so simple like a 2v1 can generate all the attacking flow you need"[23].

It is customary to see the first line of pressure from the opponent made up by two players, the importance gained by playing out from the back due to the impact of Barça led by Pep Guardiola was interpreted also, en masse and in popularity into mechanisms of playing out with three players in the first line of play. Systems with three central defenders, wide lateral movements, centre-halves, insiders or "interiores" to incorporate the furthest or deepest last line, or more recently the use of the "sweeper keeper" playing out of the goal-line at the moment of building up an attack, are different way that teams have found to res-

---

22 Fernández, Daniel (2012). *Perarnau Magazine*: The positional game. *El juego de posición*. Extracted from: **https://www.martiperarnau.com/el-juego-de-posicion/**
23 GOL (24th July, 2019). *90 minutos con Pep Guardiola*. Extracted from: **https://youtu.be/hNCjnwKEea4**

pond to when being outnumbered. "When you are starting out, the idea is to create superiority so this may allow you to break the first line of pressure of the opposition", says Eusebio Sacristán.

The ex-Spain international who played seven seasons for Fútbol Club Barcelona, and where his later coaching career has taken him to lead from the bench at Celta Vigo, Barça B, Real Sociedad or Girona, Eusebio is a manager who has taken a gamble on numerous occasions in building out play from the back with a backline of three defenders: "If they have a lone striker, with two central defenders you can outnumber because you are able to move the ball until you advance with it a few metres and move onto the next phase. If the opposition has two strikers, the answer depends on what may interest you and on the movements of pressure that may be applied in the next phase. In my case I was able to achieve by employing my pivot to drop. The objective is that one of the three players that you have in that starting line beat the first wave of pressure by the opposition"[24].

Sergi Samper played under the instructions of Eusebio at Barça B between 2013 and 2015, and as a midfielder he was in charge many times to sit deep in order to create a first step or line to allow the backline a numerical superiority to play the ball out from the back: "It is a position where I find myself comfortable because I can see the play from the front, face-on. We would do this normally at Barça B when the opposition would play us with two strikers. We would play with three to create 3v2 situations, and from there we would attempt to split and play with two central defenders or take the ball and dribble it up in order to find one of our wide midfielders, (interiores) or wing-halves"[25].

24 *En un momento dado* (2021). Interview with Eusebio Sacristán. Extracted from: https://eumd.es/2021/04/entrevista-eusebio-sacristan/

25 *En un momento dado* (2021). Interview with Sergi Samper. Extracted from: https://eumd.es/2021/04/entrevista-sergi-samper/

The construction of play from the back with three defenders also allows other types of advantages. One is in the more comfortable use of width of the pitch, by enlarging the metres that the opposition needs to defend. Pep Guardiola explains it from his experience when at Barça B, playing in the third tier, the Tercera División and on playing pitches with reduced dimensions or measurements: "At those smaller pitches, with artificial grass, it seems impossible to play out from the back, but we would achieve this by bringing in and employing the goalkeeper into play to turn or rotate the opponent. If we were able to do it at those matches, it can be done at every league and at all football pitches. You have to insist, and believe in it, because the spaces are there. Spaces do exist. The pitch to be honest, are huge, but it is us who reduce and dwarf it if we do not make good movements. But the spaces are there"[26].

On the other hand, other advantages of playing out from the back with three players has to do with the drawing in or the attraction. With the claim launched by that third player onto one of the opposing players, if that player wants to return to even out numerically then he will be forced to vacate his original space. If one of the full-backs moves to hold at the height of the centre-backs, or if one of the midfielders delays his position to sit as a fullback at the start of play, the opposition will need to extract one of the players from their midfield, thus creating a hole that the team can take advantage of to move forward. Perhaps for this reason, and although initially the formula most repeated by Guardiola had to do with holding Abidal from the side forming a sort of left centre-back alongside Gerard Piqué, Rafa Márquez o Carles Puyol, one of the variants in the script by Pep that was quickly replicated by other teams

---

26 GOL (24th July, 2019). *90 minutos con Pep Guardiola*. Extracted from: https://youtu.be/hNCjnwKEea4

that consisted in the movement in behind the midfield: the "lavolpiana" way of playing out.

Named in reference to Argentine manager Ricardo La Volpe who integrated it to his game plan at several teams, where playing out was aimed at building up numerical superiority using a pivot in the central defence zone, normally opening the positioning of the defenders so that the guest from midfield can cover the central alley or plot. "It was very common to see an opponent to press with a 1-4-4-2, with the two strikers covering the two central defenders and the wingers going with the full-backs. Therefore, when the holding midfielder as pivot drops it was very strange for the opposing pivot would follow the marker until the height of the defensive live. This was employed to create a 3v2", described Àlex Delmàs.

The "lavolpiana" way received special attention starting from the 2006 World Cup, a tournament where Ricardo La Volpe took charge of a Mexican national team squad that stood out for their neat construction of play. With a backline three made up of Rafa Márquez, Ricardo Osorio and Carlos Salcido, to start play that did not go unnoticed to the attention of Guardiola, up until then still foreign to the sideline bench: "In the match against Iran, Márquez, Osorio and Salcido were the best students in the class. The three were wonderful generating play"[27]. Pep wrote an article about them and the Mexican national side or the tricolor in the month of June for newspaper El País, where generous accolades were dedicated to the proposal of play by La Volpe and his men playing out from the back: "Ricardo La Volpe, native from Argentina and manager of the Mexican national team, have chosen its defence to play out from the back. Rather than starting out from the back, which is different. For Ricardo La Volpe, starting from the back is passing the ball between defenders, with much intention,

---

27 Guardiola, Josep (2006). *Salir de novios. El País newspaper.*

to move it side by side and then sending the ball long. For La Volpe however it forces another situation. It forces to play out from the back, where it is nothing more than involving players and the ball advancing together, in unison. If it is done alone, there is no reward, it does not count. It must be done together. Just like how it is done when a boyfriend and girlfriend go out together".

The Argentinean manager recalls himself, had carved a taste for playing out back from the back from his time as a player: "Playing out with protagonism is a great advantage. Having the ball, taking away the opponent's initiative (...) I used to be a goalkeeper, and throughout my playing career I realised it was not the same when we would go forward sending the ball long so to win a second rebound ball than when we attempted to play the ball out building up play patiently from the back. For example, I was four years with César Luis Menotti in the national team, and I observed the importance that has keeping the ball as protagonists building up from the back. In San Lorenzo I also had two coaches who would instil attempts to play out from the back: Pedernera, who had been an impressive player, and Rogelio Domínguez, who had been a goalkeeper at Real Madrid. When I became a coach, I set out to put into practice what I had learned"[28].

To achieve this, one of the fundamental aspects of his particular instruction book was related to adapting to the type of defence that the opposition puts forward, to the point of pointing out that, in part, as a coach he works to counteract the opposition's system. "I believe in the players. Without a doubt, great players make great teams, but I also believe a lot in tactical discipline. I also believe a lot in tactical discipline, in movements that will counteract the opponent who knows how to mark me". That's why, despite his affinity for the three-man attack,

---

28 *En un momento dado* (2021). Interview with Ricardo La Volpe. Extracted from: https://eumd.es/2021/04/entrevista-ricardo-la-volpe/

La Volpe believes that it makes sense against teams that press with two strikers, as against those that press with just one, the centre-back pairing finds numerical superiority without the intermediation of a third player.

Both Álvaro Benito and Àlex Delmàs also coincide, on par with a post-match wrap by Pep Guardiola when he lamented complaining why Manchester City had placed too many players behind the ball at the start of the game. The manager from Santpedor pointed out in the press room that starting the game with Stones, Kolarov and Fernando in front of a lone striker made no sense as the centre-backs were already starting from a situation of numerical superiority. Fixing a third player down low only led to the loss of a possible receiver in front of the ball.

On coming out from the back, La Volpe insists on the importance of orienting play towards the flanks ("I come out wide because I want the opposing midfielder to leave me space when he wants to press me. The width is what makes the opposition leave you space"), explaining the usefulness of fielding a player like Rafa Márquez, who is more inclined to play on the right flank: "As it was a line of three, he was almost the full-back. The right centre-back ended up being almost a full-back. And what Rafa had was a change of direction, a thirty or thirty-five metre pass with spectacular precision (...). When I had him when I was young, he had what I needed to be the centre-back, to sweep between the other two centre-backs. He was quick then. But later on, when he kept his technique but lost a bit of speed, Ricardo Osorio was the very fast one. So much so that Stuttgart signed Osorio to play at right-back.

Similarly, when, from his second year as Barça coach, Guardiola began to apply the Lavolpian approach by moving the midfield position back, first with Yaya Touré and later with Sergio Busquets, he kept his most important passers on the outside. Márquez, Piqué and, circumstantially, Dmitro Chigrinskiy, sought to give lustre to their movements with extra metres and seconds starting on the outside.

However, the period in which Guardiola most consistently shaped a construction from the back in which his midfield was embedded between the centre-backs was from the arrival of Xabi Alonso at Bayern Munich. The Spain international, who had already put the mechanism into practice at Real Madrid under José Mourinho, was more suited to this variant than other midfielders as Guardiola had managed thanks to his organisational skills and his ability to move long.

Despite its initial attraction at the start of the decade, for many the mechanism has been more of a starting point for finding alternatives than a roadmap to be followed to the letter. The fact is that the separation of the centre-backs and the fact that the player who passes between them must leave his starting position during the course of the play has sometimes been read as a vulnerability if the operation is not perfect. If the outlet fails, by the time the ball changes sides the defenders in charge of closing down the centre, and therefore the shortest and most direct access to the goal, are too far apart, away from the goalkeeper and the possibility of the striker enjoying a comfortable path through the central lane.

This is why, the list of alternatives to maintain a first tier formed by three players at the moment of getting the ball out of play is extensive. It begins with variants that support one of the two full-backs (a role in which Guardiola has employed players such as Eric Abidal or Kyle Walker), to others who prefer that the midfielder's backpedalling does not take place in the centre but on the wing. Interiors such as Frenkie de Jong at Ajax or FC Barcelona, Toni Kroos at Real Madrid, Jordan Henderson at Liverpool,

Thiago Alcántara at Bayern Munich or, occasionally, David Silva, Kevin de Bruyne and Ilkay Gündogan at Manchester City, have allowed their coaches to find numerical superiority at the back without opening up the centre of the pitch. It is the same line that has been followed by teams who, while maintaining their preference for the pivot to link up with the centre-backs, have varied their route backwards to place him to the right or left of the pair of defenders.

This is what Guardiola himself has done with the Brazilian Fernandinho, or Eusebio Sacristán, who after using Sergi Samper between the centre-backs at Barça B, as coach of Real Sociedad opted to use Asier Illarramendi on the right side of the defence: "In all of this, the characteristics of the players you have in the squad influence you. If you put the pivot in the middle, get the ball moving well and come out with one of the centre-backs, that's fine. But maybe your centre-backs are less good at passing inside than your centre-half and you are more interested in your centre-half being the one who can get those inside passes in from the wing. Because if you have moved the two opposing forwards, moved them to your left and managed to get to the right with the free pivot, from there that midfielder, who in theory has a better pass than a centre-back, is going to give you a better pass selection (...) On the inside it is easier for the strikers to press. It is more difficult for the two strikers to press wide and for the midfielder to pass through the middle. It makes more sense for the two strikers to work in a coordinated way by selecting to press to one side or the other. That is why it is a good idea for the pivot to drop to one side at that moment to get the ball out".

At the same time, and also coinciding with a new phase in which there has been a great deal of evolution in the approach of pressing forward, several teams around the world have translated the search for superiority into systems with three centre-backs. Antonio Conte with Juventus, Chelsea, Inter or the Italian national team; Louis van Gaal at the helm of the Netherlands or Manchester United; some of Julian Nagelsmann's variants in the Bundesliga or Thomas Tuchel's in Germany, France and England; and more or less long-lasting episodes at Pochettino's Tottenham, Arsène Wenger's Arsenal, Unai Emery and Mikel Arteta, or even at Klopp's Liverpool and Guardiola's Manchester City. The latter is often more closely related to Cruyff's 1-3-4-3 that Guardiola used in his last season at Barça[29].

In Spanish football, one of the standard-bearers of the system with three centre-backs has been Pablo Machín, who, after winning promotion to the Primera División with Girona, also put it into practice in the top flight at Sevilla, Espanyol and Alavés. Speaking about his motivations, in an interview with Julio Maldonado "Maldini", after pointing out the defensive security provided by the presence of a fifth defender, the Soria-born coach also stopped to point out the advantages of the formation that brings the ball out from the back and the influence of Guardiola's Barça: "I think it's a scheme that gives you a lot of possibilities when it comes to bringing the ball out. What we're doing is similar to what Guardiola did when he played with Busquets in the back, but we already play with that player in there"[30].

Jordi Guerrero, assistant to Pablo Machín at Girona, Sevilla y Barcelona, considers that the proliferation of this tactical scheme is due to being "a system that gives you many options". In the defensive section, points out Jordi, "having an extra central defender allows you to have the lanes between the centre back and full-backs better cove-

29 Quintana, Miguel (2017). Ecos del balón: *La Premier contra la defensa de tres*. The Premier League against a backline three. Extracted from: http://www.ecosdelbalon.com/2017/08/sistema-tres-centrales-claves-premier-league/

30 Mundo Maldini (14th February, 2019). *Pablo Machín y Maldini a puro fútbol*. The Sevilla manager welcomes us to the Sánchez Pizjuán. *El técnico del Sevilla nos recibe en el Sánchez Pizjuán*. Extracted from: https://youtu.be/F9kzE5wm_GI

red, because despite one of the central defenders comes out to press the striker whilst the other two full-backs can close down the spaces. Teams are perhaps attempting to attacking those inside spaces more, making the full-backs go up a lot more and the inside players go into these areas a lot. making the full-backs go up a lot and the inside players go into these areas a lot. With a defence of three centre-backs this is much better solved". In addition, the coach continues, "I think that in man-to-man pressing situations this formation is the best. Because if you're pressing with a back four, one of the full-backs has to come out very high up, whereas this way you have the two wingers up top but the three centre-backs behind".

For Guerrero, who also formed part of the technical staff under Domènec Torrent when the former assistant to Guardiola took charge of Flamengo in Brazil, when playing out "it is about adding one more player to have numerical superiority, as in the way La Volpe plays out or the way Barça does with Busquets, difference being that this way you already have that player there from the start, you don't need him to come (...). When you start with three players, either they come and press you man to man, or you always have superiority. (...) In the end you have to have someone in the middle, and that's when the spaces appear. And it's about making the most of them. When the inside player jumps at you, someone has to get in behind"[31].

The controlled ball out of defence as a starting point. As the switch that activates an extensive arsenal of variants in those who intend to carry it out, and which in turn spurs responses aimed at counteracting it. This is how Juande Ramos, a coach with almost three decades of coaching experience at Real Madrid, Sevilla, Betis, Tottenham, CSKA Moscow and Dnipro, sees it: "The start of the ball is the clearest sign that football has evolved a lot. Before, few

---

31 *En un momento dado* (2021). Interview with Jordi Guerrero. Extracted from: https://eumd.es/2021/04/entrevista-jordi-guerrero/

teams started the game with a goal kick to the defenders, but they put the ball into play with a long kick from the goalkeeper and from there the game started. Now most teams start with organised play from the defence (...). The tendency to play with the ball is disappearing"[32].

Playing out from the back, together, like brides and grooms do. A first stone that builds the game, that underpins a change of objectives and priorities that is already a trend, and that conditions the way of looking at football. Of approaching what happens in it and the interpreters in charge of giving it a voice.

---

32 *En un momento dado* (2021). Interview with Juande Ramos. Extracted from: https://eumd.es/2021/04/entrevista-juande-ramos/

CHAPTER 2

PRESSURE AS AN END TO A MEANS AND AS A PRINCIPLE

> "The most highlighting characteristic of Barça under Guardiola was not possession, but rather its conduct when without the ball"[33]
>
> JULIAN NAGELSMANN

One of the first decisions Guardiola took after his unveiling as head coach of FC Barcelona was that, while he was in charge, he would not do interviews with the media. Pep would explain himself at press conferences. Before and after matches, in front of microphones with accredited press, he would transmit his message, develop his reasoning, little by little, he would publicly showcase his football ideology. He started doing so very early on, right from the get-go at his official presentation as the Blaugrana boss, in an appearance which, over the years, has

---

33 Abril, Pitu (2017). Xavi, Nagelsmann and the comeback. *Xavi, Nagelsmann y remontada. Mundo Deportivo.*

gained traction acquiring tinges of prophecy[34]. En In it he discovered the idea of play and the team model he desired for his Barça and addressed in detail current issues where with every explanation as if he knew that with each explanation he was planting a seed.

His first appearance in front of the media served, for example, to answer questions about the club's transfer policy. In particular, the fact that most of the signings made were defenders. Dani Alves, Gerard Piqué and Martín Cáceres were the new faces in defence, leaving only Seydou Keita and Aliaksandr Hleb arrriving at the Camp Nou to strengthen other areas. "I've been reading lately that we're only signing defenders. It doesn't mean that by signing more defenders we will defend better. We will attack better if we defend well, and we will defend better if we attack well". With this last point, the link between phases and, in particular, the benefits that an effective offensive performance could bring to the team defensively, Pep was introducing very early on one of the pillars of his game plan: pressing after a loss of the ball. "The foundation of my game is in the way we defend", the coach once said[35].

Guardiola's teams' approach revolves around the ball. From the desire to keep the ball for as long as possible in order to build, from its control, the initiative in the game. It is not about turning possession of the ball into the final result, but about wanting it as a starting point. Like a speaking slot through which to speak about the match. For this reason, the immediate objective when losing the ball is to recover it. Spend as little time as possible without it. Snatching the microphone from the opponent: "When it comes to the ball, I confess I'm selfish: I want it for myself. That's why, if I don't have it, I go for it in a hurry. Know that

---

34 DeportesLD (27th April, 2012). Guardiola's presentation as coach of Barcelona.. *Así fue la presentación de Guardiola como entrenador del Barcelona*. Extracted from: https://www.youtube.com/watch?v=TYPpvRP78qE

35 Perarnau, Martí (2014). *Herr Pep. Crónica desde dentro de su primer año en el Bayern Múnich*. Barcelona, España: Editorial Córner.

I'm coming for you!"[36]. The reaction must be immediate to achieve one of Guardiola's goals: where every moment of play take place closer to the opponent's goal than our own. "When I see that the ball is closer to the opponent's goal, I am calmer, and when I see it closer to ours, I suffer more. I plan and watch the games, even when I was playing, thinking about how to cause damage to the opponent".

The idea of defending by pressing high, away from one's own penalty area, has such significant forefathers as Arrigo Sacchi's AC Milan and Rinus Michels' Dutch national side - nicknamed in Spanish "la Naranja Mecánica" or the Clockworks Orange, [37] and Pepe was able to discover it first-hand while playing under Johan Cruyff, himself a disciple of Michels. "If you want to go forward," said the architect of the Dream Team at the time, "you need people with fine technique, like Laudrup, for example, and these players perform much better on a small pitch than on a big pitch. A small pitch means that when you play in attack, Laudrup doesn't have to drop forty or fifty metres to defend and when you get the ball back, he has to go up again. When you can get him in there, the performance of players like Laudrup or Romário is much greater, and also, because they play the ball a lot, there's a lot to see. If you don't just see them running, then you see them touching the ball"[38].

Defending high up so as not to have to run backwards, reducing physical the distance of physical efforts. To bring danger to the opponent's goal quickly after winning the ball back and defend a smaller area of the pitch populated

---

36 Suárez, Orfeo (2017). Zidane and Guardiola, two ways of exerting pressure. *Zidane y Guardiola, dos formas de ejercer la presión. El Mundo.*

37 Roldán, Francisco Javier (2020). *Rinus Michels. La escuela holandesa llega al Barça.* Editorial Libro Fútbol.

38 Aquest Any, Cent! (1999). "Johan Cruyff". Televisió de Catalunya – CCMA.

39 Perarnau, Martí (2014). *Herr Pep. Crónica desde dentro de su primer año en el Bayern Múnich.* Barcelona, España: Editorial Córner.

by players of your own team. "If I have to defend this whole room, I'm the worst player there is because they can go all over me, but if I only have to defend this table, the best player in the world can come and he won't get past me. So what is good defending and what is bad defending? It's relative. It's distance, nothing more", *Cruyff illustrated in a conversation with Jorge Valdano.*

Due to the immediacy with which pressure follows the loss of the ball, and since the loss of the ball, and given that the objective is to ensure that both actions take place in the same area of the pitch, the link between the team's performance when in possession of the ball and its subsequent recovery attempts go hand in hand. Defensive organisation is a direct result of the previous offensive organisation. That is to say, if the team manages to ensure that the moment when the ball is lost, many players are close to the ball, occupying the opponent's escape routes and with the opposing players disorganised and disorientated, their chances of quickly regaining possession will be greater.

This is how Juanma Lillo explains it: "The previous events are the ones that allow you to steal the ball close to where you lose it. If the team hasn't travelled with the ball, they can't recover at the moment of the loss. If you are too far away from where you lose it, you can't go and press. You're going to make a big effort and the opponent is going to make the decision calmly. On the other hand, if we all go together, then you can go and steal. In other words, what happens when you steal the ball has to do with what has happened until you lose it".

In the same vein, Guardiola says that the secret to his team's ability to win the ball back quickly lies in the fact that "we are together. The distances between us are short. When the distance is too big, even the fastest and most physical players can't get there, because the ball is always faster than them. That's why we try to move forward together. Losing the ball after a sequence of ten, fifteen or twenty passes helps you to be closer together, and then your action is four or five metres, and you can do it immediately. When you lose the ball forty metres out, you can't get to press. The ball organises you. This is why, Guardiola concludes, "if there is no sequence of fifteen passes beforehand then it is impossible to make a good transition between attack and defence. Impossible"[39].

For Eusebio Sacristán, the recipe with which he converted Real Sociedad into one of the most dominant La Liga sides by pressing after losing the ball was similar: "The idea is that you overlap in attack, that way the positions are well occupied, covering spaces very well for when losing the ball there is always a player close to your opponent with the ball[40].

In attack, therefore, it is understood from a double point of view. As the path towards goal but, at the same time, as the preparation of a pressing scenario in which the opponent has little time to make decisions, the action is confined to a small area of the pitch and the opponent has no free path to advance"[41].

On the topic of the importance of pressure after losing the ball in team formations, as pointed out by analyst Àlex Delmàs, Guardiola's Barça represents a turning point: "They showed the world that you can play well, start play from the back cleanly and at the same time put a lot of pressure on. To go out in a controlled manner to get into the opposition's half, but once you're in you don't get out of there. To be able to make long possessions and then attack and attack again through pressure. It's a model of

---

40 *En un momento dado* (2021). Interview a Eusebio Sacristán. Extracted from: https://eumd.es/2021/04/entrevista-eusebio-sacristan/

41 Chamarro, Víctor (2019). Mis amistosos: How to work on pressure after loss? *¿Cómo trabajar la presión tras pérdida?* Extracted from: https://misamistosos.com/como-trabajar-la-presion-tras-perdida/

42 *En un momento dado* (2021). Interview with Àlex Delmàs. Extracted from: https://eumd.es/2021/04/entrevista-alex-delmas/

success, and all successful models of success you try to copy"[42].

Marcelo Bielsa as well, confessed by Guardiola as one of his most admired managers, highlights the issue of pressuring after losing the ball as one of the main contributions to Guardiola's teams to the football of his era. "I have watched in detail what Guardiola has crafted, and the key message is to defend running forwards. Is that phrase understood? You lose the ball and instead of retracting, which is the natural message, Barcelona would do the opposite: defend going forwards even further"[43].

Nevertheless, in addition to the contagion of pressure from losing the ball, there is a second issue linked to apply pressure and to the game played by teams led by Guardiola that has ended in impregnating a brand of football that has provided continuation: pressure against the opposition's start of play. In this case, it is about applying pressure that does not start from a linked situation where one of the teams loses possession and the ball goes to the other team without interruption the run of play, rather it builds up from a finished move. It does not begin from a ball recovery; it begins from an attack that dispels from the goal-line or that ends up in the hands of the goalkeeper. This is when the match takes a breather to allow both sides to recover and reorganise on the field of play.

Time ago, when this occurred, it was common to see sides move around further away to the middle of the pitch. The defending team would do this with the objective of taking positions close to goal this way avoiding the opposition to get to goal; meanwhile the team attacking searches for a better willingness to fight for the ball by sending it directly

---

43 Medarde, Francisco [@futbolxvenas] (18th January, 2020). Defending by running forward was a thing that didn't exist. Do you understand that phrase? *Defender corriendo hacia delante era una cosa que no existía. ¿Entienden esa frase?* [Tweet]. Twitter. **https://twitter.com/futbolxvenas/status/1218387531210903552**

44 Moñino, Ladislao (2017). High pressing, Atlético's antidote against Barcelona. *La presión alta, el antídoto del Atlético contra el Barcelona. El País.*

long from the goalkeeper or from one of the defenders. Starting from the second decade of the 21st century, albeit, as a result from the build-up of playing out with short passes, and from a better execution by teams to employ a deep-sitting defensive system, the prevailing tendency has shifted to the construction of very advanced pressing systems, also when the opposing team starts the game from their own area. Arrigo Sacchi said this at the beginning of 2017 in a conversation with Carlo Ancelotti: "Recently we were talking about this tendency to press high (...) we concluded that in Italy teams are still well organised at the back, but that in Europe this more attacking trend was becoming more prevalent"[44].

When there are practically all ten on-field players defending in blocks defending beyond the dividing halfway line, this leaves a great amount of metres behind their backs thus forcing their efforts in cutting down the first attacking links by the opponent. In fact, on many occasions, raising a man-by-man match-up across the pitch. Applying individual marking to each and every opposing player, the way Adrián Cervera analyses in his work as coach, scout, sporting director and teacher of the CEDIFA Methodology[45], regarding the approach to the game[46], project different challenges to those posed by more zonal pressure models: "When the opposition When the opposition would pressure you in a zone, the fundamental thing was to have numerical superiority on the line where the ball was to find a free man and attack intervals between defenders and between lines, and thus break those lines of containment. But now, if they press you and mark you man-to-man, there are no lines of containment but duels"[47]. When the pressure prioritises individual pursuit over zonal cover,

---

45 Centro de Estudios, Desarrollo e Investigación del Fútbol Andaluz.

46 Cervera, Adrián (2020). The approach game. *El juego de aproximación*. España.

47 *En un momento dado* (2021). Interview with Adrián Cervera. Extracted from: https://eumd.es/2021/04/entrevista-adrian-cervera/

the possibility of finding an unmarked team-mate vanishes. Each player has his own bodyguard.

"Teams have realised that the best way, and also the least risky way, of being able to stay close to the opposing goal is to press high up," says Àlex Delmàs. "They prefer to leave space at the back in exchange for being able to recover high up the pitch". Teams that group together in blocks further forward to start pressing the opponent's ball from very high up, facing the general desire to come out playing short, taking advantage of any committed turnovers that because they occur close to the goal, can easily translate into a dangerous chance, and preventing the opponent from getting into promising attacking positions.

It is a development that Adrián Cervera describes as follows: "Early in the year 2000 very zonally defensive teams emerged. With two lines very compact, bringing in the strikers into the defensive phase, where they group up close to the area or the middle zone and were successful because in those days the offensive processes were not that very well developed. Teams were much more direct. Starting from 2008 Guardiola began to break down all those systems by giving them a shake-up by way of positional play, from the creation of superiority from the back, from the occupation of spaces between lines... and that was creating a school and it was becoming increasingly difficult for teams to defend by being reactive againsnst a side that would play and treat the ball well". Not for nothing Juan Carlos Unzué, member of the technical staff of Guardiola at Barcelona, noted at the time that "something that Pep does differently to other coaches is his ability to analyse the game tactically, but unlike most coaches, not only defensively but also offensively"[48].

---

48 Sportyou (1st September, 2010). Unzué: "Guardola is different to the rest". *"Guardiola es diferente al resto"*. Extracted from: https://youtu.be/ql8V5v-4jek

As one of them started to go forward making things difficult with positional play," Cervera continued, "little by little everyone else started to move their defensive blocks forward. Nowadays 90% of the top teams try to play out from the back, and the best way to counteract this and do more damage to this type of team is to press high".

Guardiola's Barça, then, in a way, was the trigger for a new golden age of high pressing from two almost opposing points of view. From the point of view of those who tried to imitate him and incorporated into their game an aspect such as pressing after loss. And also from the point of view of those who tried to respond to his contagion by confronting pressure with the will to start generating advantages from the beginning of the game. But while their paths advanced together, neither Pep nor the Blaugrana of Barcelona had to face up to the pressure of their opponents, as they did later on separately. Although the Santpedor-born coach said on more than one occasion that he preferred to play against opponents who stayed back and defended close to goal rather than against teams who opted to press him up front, the truth is that the general tendency against Barça between 2008 and 2012 was to retreat.

As a consequence of the advantage then gained by their ball delivery over the defensive responses in the form of advanced defending that their opponents generally concluded that moving forward and moving away from their own goal was a risk with very little guarantee of paying off.

In this respect, one of the most illustrative chapters is that of Cristiano Ronaldo in the first leg of the Champions League semi-finals of the 2010-2011 season, when Real Madrid, led by Portuguese manager José Mourinho, took on Guardiola's Barça at the Santiago Bernabéu. Mourinho's tactics prioritised that, when the blaugranas had the ball, Madrid would stay back, occupying with many men the space where Messi, Xavi and Andrés Iniesta could appear, and avoiding a comfortable performance by Barça's three youth players at all costs. Real Madrid, meanwhile, in order not to separate their lines, would only press the start of build-up play of their rival at selected moments, assuming that the team would spend many minutes of play without the ball and far from the goalmouth defended that night by Víctor Valdés. The Catalan goalkeeper, in the end, completed more passes than any Madrid player except Xabi Alonso.

Against this backdrop, during a period of possession in which Barça circulated the ball between the centre-backs and the midfield, Cristiano Ronaldo opted to attempt a recovery, advance his defensive position and harass the ball-winner. Seeing himself overrun and realising that his team-mates behind him had not followed him but had kept a low defence, the Portuguese could not restrain an ostensible gesture of disapproval, later reaffirmed in front of the microphones: "I don't like playing like this, but I have to adapt"[49].

A month and a day later, Manchester United would succumb in the Champions League final against Messi, Xavi, Iniesta, Busquets, Dani Alves, Pedro, David Villa and Co. The only goal for the English side was scored by Wayne Rooney, who had previously shared a dressing room with Cristiano Ronaldo for five years at United and who, in his subsequent analysis of the match, seemed to be more in tune with the strategy Mourinho employed at the Bernabéu than with Alex Ferguson and his former team-mate: "We lost two finals against FC Barcelona under Guardiola

---

49 ABC (2011). Cristiano Ronaldo: "I don't like playing like that, but I have to adapt". Cristiano Ronaldo: *No me gusta jugar así, pero tengo que adaptarme*". *ABC*.

trying to press high. It was suicidal (...) I think all the players knew that, in the end, it was the wrong approach"[50].

Regarding the risks the teams took when they tried to press Guardiola's Barça, Adrián Cervera recalls in particular a duel between the Culés and Sevilla under Manolo Jiménez: "It was one of the first times a team came out to put pressure on Guardiola's Barça. It ended 4-0, but it could have ended 10-0 down if Barça had wanted to". Adrián believes that "they were used to zonal references, and because Barça had so much quality, they always ended up playing out. That's why they didn't normally press as much, because the mechanisms to make the pressures more effective weren't the same as they are now. It wasn't until 2015 or 2016 that teams started to dominate it well".

Unzué confirms this when he recalls that in his last year at Barça, as part of Luis Enrique's coaching staff, they detected a change in the way opponents played against them: "When we were playing our 40th official game of the season, do you know how many teams had put us under high pressure, including pressure on the goalkeeper? Twenty-six teams out of forty (...) Suddenly, coaches who had always been more of a retreat, dared to give us that high pressure. When that happens, it's because they feel they can get something out of it and that they are putting you in difficulty. There has been a very big progression over the years"[51].

In the same vein says Álvaro Benito, who also points out that "there is no team in the world today that is capable of having the kind of possession that Guardiola's Barça or the Spanish national team had (...), opponents were unable to steal a ball from them. And that's what the pressu-

---

50 Sport (2020). Rooney calls Ferguson's tactics in Champions League finals 'suicidal'. *"Rooney califica de "suicidas" las tácticas de Ferguson en las finales de Champions 2009 y 2011"*. Sport.

51 *En un momento dado* (2021). Interview with Juan Carlos Unzué. Extracted from: https://eumd.es/2021/04/entrevista-juan-carlos-unzue/

res have been taking advantage of. There was a time when many believed that they were Guardiola's Barça and that everyone could play like Guardiola's Barça, but that was a lie (...). In my opinion, pressure on playing out with the ball is gaining the upper hand. There are very few teams that come out on top of pressures like Liverpool or Getafe, teams that press in a continuous, aggressive and very determined and organised way"[52].

Pep Guardiola himself, now out of Barça, has also seen how little by little the favourite recipe by rival coaches playing against his teams have turned to prioritising high pressure over more retreat-oriented approaches. "He has experienced this more in England than in Germany", says Martí Perarnau. Over the course of his three seasons in the Bundesliga, teams such as Mainz under Thomas Tuchel or, especially Borussia Dortmund under Jürgen Klopp, faced Guardiola with ferocious high-end pressure, but the formula ended up the norm after his arrival in the Premier League. "He has encountered this much more in England, where this evolution has already taken place and high pressure is quite common in many teams", explained Martí Perarnau.

Apart from Guardiola, another guiding thread linking the German Bundesliga with the English Premier League: Jürgen Klopp took charge of the sidelines at Liverpool only a season before Pep arrived at Etihad Stadium. The arrival of the German manager to Anfield, thus, made the Premier League a duel for the two managers, a battle initially framed around the teams under Guardiola and Klopp but which, due to both teams' track record in the competition, has since taken on a global and contextual translation.

En primer lugar, como antes el Bayern o el Barcelona, la incontestable temporada 2017-18 del Manchester City

---

52 *En un momento dado* (2021). Interview with Álvaro Benito. Extracted from: https://eumd.es/2021/04/entrevista-alvaro-benito/

señaló el rival a batir. El listón al que adaptarse. La vara de medir. Hasta 27 récords batieron aquel curso los citizen, incluyendo los de puntos, victorias, diferencia respecto al segundo clasificado, goles a favor y en contra, o número de rivales vencidos[53]. Durante nueve meses, Inglaterra no halló la respuesta a las nuevas preguntas que le planteaba el equipo de Guardiola a través de las botas de Silva, De Bruyne, Sterling, Sané, Fernandinho o el Kun Agüero. No fue hasta el curso siguiente que el fútbol inglés creyó haber descubierto el antídoto, a pesar del nuevo título de liga skyblue, gracias a un Liverpool que, bajo la batuta de Klopp, quedó a un solo punto del líder. El fútbol del entrenador alemán, basado en la presión (el gegenpressing[54]) como el arma más eficaz contra la propuesta del campeón, subrayada por los posteriores éxitos reds y exportada al mundo gracias a los acaparadores focos de la Premier League[55].

"Liverpool under Klopp is the most difficult opponent I have encountered in my career as coach. The team I've had the hardest time cracking"[56], , said Pep during the run for the 2019-20 season title. It is not for nothing that the German is, of all the coaches Guardiola has faced, the one with the best record against the Catalan. Pep argues that "when you have a good outlet for the ball, the rest flows much more naturally"[57], that superiority in the first pass is the key to the superiority that will come later, so that a model of play like Klopp's, based on high pressing from

---

53 Aguilar, Bernat (2018). "Pep Guardiola's 27 records at Manchester City." "*Los 27 nuevos récords que regala Pep Guardiola al Manchester City*". *El Nacional.*

54 Counterpressure. *Contrapresión.*

55 Carey, Mark (2020). Tableau Public: Pressing Styles across European Top 5 Leagues. Recuperado de: https://public.tableau.com/profile/mark.carey#!/vizhome/ EuropeanPressingStyles/PressuresDashboard

56 Blanco, Eugenio (2020). Guardiola on DAZN: "Klopp's Liverpool is the opponent I've had the hardest time deciphering". "*El Liverpool de Klopp es el rival al que más me ha costado descifrar*". *GOAL.*

57 GOL (24th July, 2019). 90 minutos con Pep Guardiola. Extracted from: https:// youtu.be/hNCjnwKEea4

the start of play, represents a threat directly launched on one of the core principles of his football[58].

On the structural value of pressing in Liverpool's game, both defensively and offensively the most graphic comment was made by Jürgen Klopp himself, stating that pressing forward can have the effects of the best midfield playmaker, equating the damaging potential of a recovery close to the box with the iconic figure more associated with attacking creativity and the ability to generate dangerous chances[59]. "The most important thing is for the players to understand how important it is for our team to put pressure on our opponents' ball playing out from the back", explains Pepijn Lijnders, one of Klopp's assistants at Liverpool. "They have to feel it, not with their heads but with their hearts"[60].

One of Klopp's most gifted pupils is Sadio Mané, who from the forward line is part of the first wave the Reds launch against their opponents when the latter try to build an advantage from the ball: "It depends on when the opponents give a certain pass and who they give it to. That's the signal for everyone... Nobody gives a voice. We know in which situations to press and in which situations to retreat and come together. It's about reading the opponent. You don't need a team-mate to go after him. When you see that the opponent makes a certain pass, you don't need to look back. You know 100% that all your teammates will move behind you. It is the opponent who gives you the tempo depending on how and with whom they play the ball. This is a little secret. But I can say that

---

58 Sports Nova (2020). Gegenpressing vs Tiki-taka: The philosophical difference between Jürgen Klopp and Pep Guardiola. Recuperado de: https://www.sports-nova. com/2020/02/15/gegenpressing-vs-tiki-taka-the-philosophical-difference-be-tween-jurgen-klopp-and-pep-guardiola/

59 Moñino, Ladislao (2019). 'Fútbol tormenta', the paradigm of Jürgen Klopp. 'Fútbol tormenta', el paradigma de Jürgen Klopp. El País.

60 Renard, Arthur (2020). "At Liverpool our pressing comes from the heart". "En el Liverpool presionamos con el corazón". El País.

the tempo of our pressing movements is set by the opponent rival"[61].

Pressing seen from both sides of the glass. Firstly, from the direct influence of Guardiola's teams, as a consequence of attacking play. Later, as a cause of the same, as a product of the ascendancy that the most successful recipes have had against this approach to the game. From finding pressure through play, to finding play through pressure. Forward pressing conceived not only as the result of effective attacking play, but also as a form of offensive organisation in itself[62].

The coming out from the back and pressing, two fundamental aspects of the game and twinned in post-2010 football, that have changed both the development of matches and their analysis or preparation. "If both teams try to play out from the back and both try to press, that's where the game is born. That's the germ of it," stresses Adrián Cervera. To win that battle is to face the rest with superiority, conditioning the duel from the first advantageous move. That's why, in search of the best preparation to achieve victory, the training sessions of the teams' training sessions have had to adapt to such a particular scenario.

Pressure "is an element that is present in every exercise", affirmed Lijnders on newspaper El País. "I take charge of training sessions. It's very simple. It has to do with continually stimulating the desire to win back the ball the quickest time and the furthest and highest possible on the pitch (...), you will hear me, you will hear Jürgen or Pete scream: 'Go on! Recover the ball! Don't stop!' You could even hear us in Manchester. They have to understand why it is so important".

---

61 Torres, Diego (2018). Sadio Mané: "Playing the Play Station is a waste of time for nothing". *"Jugar a la Play Station es perder el tiempo a cambio de nada". El País.*

62 Ustáriz, Eduardo (2020). Can you win the Champions League without pressing forward? *¿Se puede ganar la Champions sin presionar adelante? El Espectador.*

High pressure as a global phenomenon. Firstly as a result of the increasing reliance on the controlled start from the back that followed the influence of Guardiola's Barça, then because of the role played in the interantional scene by coaches such as Klopp, Tuchel, Rangnick, Hasenhüttl or Nagelsmann, who fed and lived the evolution first-hand in the Bundesliga and, finally, for the way the exposure of the Premier League exports the recipe.

And as football doesn't stop, what was once an adaptation to the rise and growth of playing out from the back, has now become the need to adjust to the scenario posed by the pressures. A scenario in which the location of the available spaces changes, as well as the type of actions that are easier to execute in the different areas of the pitch. A scenario that invites you to run if you get past the first challenge, with the midfielders launching in transition ("Now I have Kevin de Bruyne, who is a beast running after winning the ball back"[63]), and that uncovers free areas behind the opposing defences. Now we play in big spaces," says Álvaro Benito, "the tendency is to run, to attack big spaces, to stretch the team as much as possible, to attack forward, constantly breaking lines, and to attack in a few seconds. For me, broadly speaking, the change in recent years has been there. We have moved from small spaces to big spaces".

This is probably why more teams are discovering that the long pass is a particularly useful resource. First of all, because it is a solution that allows you to avoid the problem posed by the advanced pressure on the short passes: they move the ball to the back of the pressure without having to face it directly. And secondly, because through the long movement and the technique that goalkeepers and centre-backs have used over the last decade to execute it, they activate the areas of the pitch where their opponents

---

63 GOL (24th July, 2019). 90 minutos con Pep Guardiola. Extracted from: https://youtu.be/hNCjnwKEea4

have fewer players and where they are therefore more vulnerable.

As Álvaro Benito points out: "You have to be prepared because that's where the space is. When you're in the front line, the opposing team stretches (...), if the opponent has six players, there will be a 4v4 in the other area of the pitch in a very advantageous situation if I keep that ball. In the years that I've been coaching I've always tried to make sure that the players are able to identify different situations (...) everything is caused by forward pressure".

After the debut of Aymeric Laporte at Manchester City for example, opposing manager Alan Pardew was quick to announce how beneficial it would be for Guardiola's team to have a centre-back with the Frenchman's long delivery ability: "His pass from left to right was a problem for us. I have bad news for the Premiership: City have another resource, not only defensively but offensively as well. Good luck to the rest"[64]. On that day, the centre-back made his debut in the English Premier League with a 95 per cent passing success rate and a total of 76 successfully complete passes served.

Adrián Cervera continues on the same thread, when he notes how "one of Liverpool's big changes has been the dominance of the long pass. The change of direction from one flank to the other and the deliveries from the back of the last line are fundamental to their success. It's a team that uses a lot of switching forward and sending behind the back of the defence to take advantage of Salah and Mané."

It is the necessary utility of full-backs like Trent Alexander-Arnold or Andrew Robertson, centre-backs like Van Dijk, Laporte, Bastoni or Sergio Ramos, midfielders like

---

64 Ballús, Pol (2018). Laporte makes a winning debut for City. *Laporte debuta con nota con el City. Sport.*

Kroos, Kimmich or Thiago Alcántara, and goalkeepers like Ederson, Ter Stegen or Manuel Neuer, in response to a football conditioned and chiselled by the forward pressing that most teams play. A football born to combat those who reign in the opponent's area thanks to the way they initiate the game from their own.

CHAPTER 3

GOALKEEPER FROM HEAD TO TOE

> "I think the next evolution of football will come when the goalkeeper is involved in attacking play. The coach who has the courage to do that will be the one who will attack best"[65]
>
> PEP GUARDIOLA

On the 28th of May 2011, Fútbol Club Barcelona conquered their fourth European Cup in their history on the famous Wembley turf by an imposing a 3-1 victory over Manchester United. *Sir* Alex Ferguson was on his nineteenth season at the helm of the *Red Devils*, later admitted that the Cup Final loss at the hands of Guardiola, Messi, Xavi, Iniesta, Piqué, Dani Alves, Busquets, and Co had been the most resounding defeat ever suffered by his team. "Nobody had given us a beating like that. They enjoy football. During my time as football manager, I would

---

65 LaTdT (2020). Let's talk about football. *Parlem de Futbol*. Corporació Catalana de Mitjans Audiovisuals.

have to say that that was the best team I had come up against"[66].

Although Barça had conceded a goal in the 34th minute and equalised, it was a dominating display from start to finish. Their uncontested choral play with the triangle formed by Xavi Hernández, Andrés Iniesta, and Leo Messi deep into the heartbeat of the final where they held the English side at bay. They were exposed by the virtues of each *Blaugrana* footballer very much to the potential they achieved when interacting with their teammates on the pitch.

Given the superior performance by Barcelona, veteran United goalkeeper Edwin van der Sar, was forced to make eight full-stretched saves to avoid a heavier defeat on his farewell season to his active playing career. On the other end, Víctor Valdés did not have to respond with his hands on any occasion with exception to the equalising goal scored by Wayne Rooney and on two occasions in the 18-yard box to intercept a pass heading towards his opposing forward.

For the Catalan goalkeeper, the final on this occasion looked far less busy in comparison to previous editions played in 2006 and in 2009 protecting the Blaugrana goal, by contributing decisively with memorable victories.

Under the Paris sky, five years earlier, Víctor had lifted his first Champions League title after himself describing it as "the night of his career"[67], keeping his side under Frank Rijkaard afloat and where Ronaldinho, Deco and Eto'o headed the side in attack. Saving a one-on-one against Thierry Henry of Arsenal, he deflected two shots by "Titi" from outside the 18-yard box, also in the second half by Ljungberg and blocking a shot by the aforementioned

---

66 Rodríguez, José María (2011). Ferguson: "No one has ever beaten us up like this before". *Nadie nos había dado una paliza así"*. *Marca*.

67 Marlon Becerra Entrevista (2015). Interview with Víctor Valdés. TV Colombia (RCN Internacional)

French striker when he had left Puyol and Rafa Márquez behind. The native goalkeeper from L'Hospitalet held his own until the final stages of the match as both Eto'o and Belletti managed to pull two goals back in reply from the opener scored by Sol Campbell.

In Rome, meanwhile, in a magical spring of 2009 that Guardiola's Barça immortalised with the first treble in the club's history, Víctor Valdés repeated his role as hero, appearing decisively to thwart Cristiano Ronaldo's chances.

While his saves in the final at Wembley in 2011 were direct responses to the scarce goal opportunities for Manchester United, so it would be inaccurate to conclude that his performance was memorable. As it is customary to say in these cases, the superiority of Barça was so evident that they may have played the final without a goalkeeper. The link the goalkeeper had with the match that unfolded and the type of game played was close, although on this occasion, it was different to the one he had had in previous matches: it moved away from his hands to his feet. Víctor Valdés did not make any saves, but he did participate as another player in his team's dominance of the ball. As a fulcrum behind the centre-backs and always offering an open outlet for possession while the ball was in play, the Barça goalkeeper intervened with his feet on the ball 17 times, a notably higher figure than the eleven times he did so in the final in Rome, and almost three times more than the mere six interventions with his feet in 2006 against Arsenal.

Nevertheless, the most memorable episode in the Champions League title won by Barça, on the topic on the impact of their goalkeeper playing with the feet, it is probably worth looking at the game that took Guardiola's side to the final at Wembley.

It was the second leg of the semi-final between the *Culés* and Real Madrid, after a first leg in which two Leo Messi goals had put the tie very much in the balance for the Catalans, when with the score level at 0-0 Mourinho's side moved forward to press a goal kick taken short by Valdés to Javier Mascherano. In the face of Madrid's pressure, the "little boss" or *el Jefecito*"as nicknamed returned to the ball to his goalkeeper who, with his first touch, sent a right-footed shot in the direction of Dani Alves with which Barça would beat up to five rival players, and which proved to be the start of the move with which Pedro Rodríguez would seal their place in the final.

The Canary Islander would acknowledge this with a wink from afar, and so would Pep Guardiola who celebrated the goal by pointing his two index fingers at this goalkeeper. "Guardiola has brought us to this final. He has always taught us this was way of playing. The goal was his creation. What they tell us we try to put into practice, and it worked out well. Hence my gesture of dedicating it to the bench"[68], as the goalkeeper would later finish off in front of the microphones. Víctor was no longer just the goalkeeper who could prevent an opponent's goal, but now he could be the source of his team's goals. His importance was no longer solely linked to the ultimate responsibility of preventing defeat and was extended to include the power to bring victory closer. The goalkeeper was there not only to not lose the match, but also to win it.

It was 2011 and Guardiola was enjoying a Valdés who had reminisced when two years earlier, just after taking charge at Barça, he called the goalkeeper into his office to convey his intentions about his place in the team. Pep explained to the goalkeeper that the Barça he wanted to build would start playing from him, and that when he had the ball the centre-backs would be positioned in the wide areas. Víctor said that he replied: "Well, let them want it, because to be there you have to want it. They have to dare.

---

68 Martín, Luís (2011).The goal by Guardiola. *El gol de Guardiola. El País.*

Guardiola answered: "Don't worry, that's what I'm going to do, make sure they want it. And that's where it all began"[69].

Not surprisingly, Willy Caballero, who coincided with the Catalan coach at Manchester City, says that "to play with Pep you had to know how to tackle and play with your feet".[70] The Argentine, was a member of the Citizens' squad before the arrival of Guardiola to the club, and had also made himself regular starter ahead of Claudio Bravo, against all odds, in the final stretch of season 2016-17. The former FC Barcelona goalkeeper was Guardiola's first choice when he arrived to the Premier League, had initially arrived in England to replace Joe Hart who was the England national team goalkeeper and the boss between the posts for City for six years, but whose characteristics, especially in terms of his footwork, were far from what Guardiola was looking for. Bravo, on the other hand, had the experience of his two seasons at Barça ("they don't want a goalkeeper who lives in the 6-yard box, stuck between the posts only making saves (...), you must be an extra player on the field"[71]) where he had successfully completed 84% of his passes in the previous season, compared to 53% for a Hart who, as a result, had given possession to the opposition more than twice as often as the Chilean[72].

Frans Hoek, who throughout his career has trained goalkeepers at Ajax, FC Barcelona, Bayern Munich, Manchester United or both the Dutch and Polish national teams, finds a parallel between the change in goal at Manchester City and the one that took place at Barcelona in 1997, with the arrival of Louis van Gaal to the Camp Nou:

---

69 Duncan McMath, Graham Hunter, Marc Guillén and Víctor M. Gros (2018). *Take The Ball Pass The Ball*. Zoomsport International.

70 Muglia, Vicente (2018). "You should never stop learning". "*Nunca tenés que dejar de aprender*". *Olé newspaper*.

71 Martín, L. and Ballús, P. (2018), *Cuaderno de Mánchester*. Barcelona, España: Malpaso Ediciones.

72 Lowe, Sid (2016). Claudio Bravo: The reluctant goalkeeper who became Pep Guardiola's No1 man. *The Guardian*.

"When we arrived, we knew that Vitor Baía was an impressive goalkeeper, but with a different profile. The issue was if it would be possible, he adapts to our way of playing. It turned out impossible. It wasn't his fault, but rather his style of play was different. We saw him very fast (...). Between Ruud Hesp and Baía everybody thought that Baía would play, but because they didn't have the model of play in mind (...) Vitor Baía was a more traditional goalkeeper and less prepared to play out from the back or anticipating, closing down spaces (...). It was a similar case with Joe Hart at Manchester City. He was the England national team goalkeeper, but he did not have the characteristics the way Pep wanted to play"[73].

It was not the first time in football history to bring the goalkeeper into play as a key and decisive element of attacking football based on the ability to play the ball with the feet[74]. It was not, however, until the second decade of the 2000s had its influence been global and pervasive. It is from then on, that the goalkeeper is understood differently in relation to his or her handling of the ball.

Thus, one of the most marked developments in the goalkeeping position since 2009 has been its increasingly clear and widespread involvement in the offensive performance of teams through their participation in playing the ball with their feet. As if the goalkeeper was just another player on the field, and assuming that the particularities that differentiate them from the rest in the regulations do not represent a limit but an addition. Far from the old patterns in which goalkeepers even handed over to an outfield player to take a goal kick, the goalkeeper is allowed to carry out each and every one of the actions that teammates are allowed to do with the added privilege of being able

---

73 *En un momento dado* (2021). Interview with Frans Hoek. Extracted from: https://eumd.es/2021/04/entrevista-frans-hoek/

74 Ustáriz, Eduardo (2015). *Ecos del balón*: With gloves and in a crazy way. *Con guantes y a lo loco*. Extracted from: http://www.ecosdelbalon.com/2015/02/analisis-porteros-liberos-rene-higuita-manuel-neuer-evolucion/

to touch the ball with the hands inside the box. The goalkeeper cannot do less than other players, the goalkeeper can do more. Jon Pascua Ibarrola, goalkeeper coach at teams including Betis, Athletic Bilbao or FC Barcelona, sums it up as follows: "I understand the goalkeeper as an outfield player who can hold the ball with the hands in a given area"[75].

Because the relevance of goalkeepers in playing the ball with their feet has to do with their involvement in the construction of the game, the attributes required of them are not technical but encompass a broader perspective of the game. The technical and shooting abilities are necessary, and generally as essential, as Marc-André ter Stegen pointed out when he acknowledged that he would not have landed at Barça if he had not been able to play with his feet[76], but since it is placed at the service of good development of attacking play, it cannot be separated from a correct reading and interpretation of game situations. The decision that first begins to define play is that of the goalkeeper[77].

Few cases exemplify this issue better than the change in goalkeeping at Levante Unión Deportiva where Oier Olazábal was given the regular starting spot, after eleven rounds in La Liga, during season 2017-2018. This is how the former Barça B goalkeeper retold events: "We were suffering a lot with the ball and the coach wanted us to have the ball more, because we were giving it away (...). We were in a bad dynamic with the ball and we tried to change that, opening up the centre-backs more, bringing the pivot down to come out (...). It is clear that what I learnt in Bar-

---

75 beIn SPORTS España (2019, junio 13). LaLiga Docs | The goalkeeper: the evolution of the specialist. *El portero: La evolución del especialista.* Extracted from: https://www.youtube.com/watch?v=8rSpHx3AZgA

76 Revista *Panenka* (2018). Ter Stegen:"I wouldn't be here if I didn't know how to play with my feet". *"No estaría aquí si no supiera jugar con los pies".* Panenka.

77 Perarnau, Martí (2016), *Pep Guardiola. La metamorfosis.* Barcelona, España: Editorial Córner.

celona gives me more resources when the coach asks you to do something else to start the game from the back"[78].

Similarly, regarding Ederson Moraes, for example, Guardiola said in a press conference that he knew "his passing ability, but he also reads very well where to give the ball"[79]. The Brazilian goalkeeper shares Ter Stegen's beginnings outside the goal as an outfield player, an aspect whose value Juan Carlos Unzué underlines in making the keeper feel like another player, recalling his move to Johan Cruyff's Barça after a play-off between the Spain and Netherlands Under-21 teams:

"I have no doubt that what they picked up on was my idea of the game. My positioning with regard to the game. And they saw that with that positioning it would be much easier for me to develop their idea. This is where I'm going to tell you why I had those qualities. It's very simple: I had these qualities because until I was fifteen years old, I alternated as an outfield player and as a goalkeeper. I felt I was already a player at that time. Until 1984 I played as a goalkeeper and as a player, and I signed for FC Barcelona en 1988"[80].

Another of the modern-day benchmarks in the position, the Brazilian Alisson Becker, on the other hand, never moved from goal, although the Liverpool goalkeeper developed his game with his feet during his years in Italy with AS Roma[81].

As the role of the goalkeeper in the team's game has changed, and consequently the actions and virtues required of him to carry them out successfully have changed,

78 Arroyo, Natalia (2018). Oier Olazábal: "I was left with my spine, I was very close". "*Vaig quedar-me amb l'espina, vaig estar-hi molt a prop*". *Ara.*

79 Ballús, Pol (2018). Ederson Moraes, or playing with Koeman as a goalkeeper. *Ederson Moraes, o jugar con Koeman de portero. Sport.*

80 En un momento dado (2021). Interview with Juan Carlos Unzué. Extracted from: https://eumd.es/2021/04/entrevista-juan-carlos-unzue/

81 López, Marcos (2018). Alisson, the hands of modernity. *Allison, las manos de la modernidad. El Periódico de Catalunya.*

the training sessions have also had to adapt to the new reality of the position. "What we can't do is demand that the goalkeeper makes good decisions and takes all these responsibilities on Sunday, but during the week let him train all the time alone with his specific goalkeeping coach", defends Unzué. "The focus has shifted to working on real situations, in real space, with pressures similar to those that the opponent will put on you, so that through practice you can improve your skills"[82]. Luis Llopis is of the same opinion, a goalkeeper coach who has worked in the technical staff of Athletic Bilbao, Mallorca, Levante, Granada, Real Madrid, or Real Sociedad, when he points out that the aim should be to "be fair to the goalkeeper, demanding correct responses to trained game situations"[83].

Frans Hoek's experience working with goalkeepers at big clubs for three decades, also serves to trace the way in which training sessions have adapted to an era that expects different things from goalkeepers. An era that does not see goalkeepers as a distinct element of the whole, but as a cog in the collective machine:

"I always think about the match and, as a consequence, training has to be like a match. You must train the way you play. That's why it's important to cooperate with the team head coach. What has changed is that when I started out, I used to do about 50% of the exercises without the participation of other players, and now I do more and more goalkeeper training with other players. I use less and less isolated exercises and I prefer to use more exercises adapted to real game situations. In 2014, at Manchester United, a maximum of 20% of goalkeeping training was done without players. The other 80% was with players".

---

82 The Coaches' Voice en español (22nd July, 2019). Clase Magistral: Juan Carlos Unzué. The role of the goalkeeper at Barcelona, from Cruyff to Luis Enrique. *El rol del portero en el Barcelona, desde Cruyff a Luis Enrique.* Extracted from: https://www.youtube.com/watch?v=mYD15XrztDQ&feature=emb_title

83 beIn SPORTS España (13th June, 2019). LaLiga Docs | The goalkeeper: The evolution of the specialist. *El portero: La evolución del especialista.* Extracted from: https://www.youtube.com/watch?v=8rSpHx3AZgA

The prelude to this change of conception regarding the place of goalkeepers in the game can be found in the back-pass rule, introduced in 1992, after which the goalkeeper could no longer pick up a pass with the hands from a team-mate with the foot without the referee punishing the action with an indirect free kick[84]. The measure was intended to avoid time-wasting situations such as those experienced in the 1990 World Cup, where teams with a favourable score systematically touched towards the goalkeeper's hands when the opponent tried to take the ball away from them[85].

For goalkeepers at the time it was generally not a welcome rule, as it was understood that it would make their job more difficult and even have the opposite effect on the game than intended, making it less spectacular as it was felt that without the goalkeeper's support, defenders would choose to clear the ball out of the hands with an uncontrolled clearance. "We are goalkeepers, not players"[86], complained Valencia goalkeeper José Manuel Sempere, unwittingly anticipating the future impact of the new rule on the position.

Santiago Cañizares, goalkeeper for the Spanish national team at the Barcelona Olympics in 1992 where the new rules were applied for the first time, recalls:

"At the beginning, in the following seasons, the defenders tried not to play with the goalkeeper because they knew he was a player with deficiencies playing with the feet. They only played with the goalkeeper when there was no other

---

84 Downer, Osmond (1997). FIFA.com: Goalkeepers are not above the rules. *Los porteros no están por encima de las reglas*. Extracted from: **https://es.fifa.com/news/los-porteros-estan-por-encima-las-reglas-76089**

85 Relaño, Alfredo (2016). No handing over to the keeper. *Prohibido ceder al portero (1992). AS.*

86 Turner, Graham (1992). Goalkeepers consider the rule banning them from using their hands to be very negative. *Los porteros consideran muy negativa la norma que les prohibe usar las manos. El País*

87 *En un momento dado* (2021). Interview with Santi Cañizares. Extracted from: https://eumd.es/2021/04/entrevista-santi-canizares/

option, and we were ordered to take the ball away from us. We had the order to take the ball away from us. (...) It didn't matter where the ball went. Then, little by little, we started to realise that it wasn't necessary to send the ball out of play and that it was possible to contest the ball. That was in the beginning, and it was a big change because it meant that the goalkeepers had to start acting differently.

All this has evolved and today the new generations come with a brutal mastery of the foot. From the age of seven or eight they train with their feet as well as with their hands. I experience this with my son, who is 17 years old and is also a football goalkeeper. When I see his teammates pass him the ball, I suffer a lot (...), but he solves these situations without any problem. I was incapable of resolving them because I didn't learn to play the ball from a young age like he did. It wasn't until I was 22 that I was taught to appreciate that you had to play with your foot"[87].

In the same vein, Frans Hoek believes that no other rule has had a greater influence on the goalkeeping game, although he points out that even before 1992, in the late 1960s, he worked along these lines with Johan Cruyff at Ajax Amsterdam:

"When the goalkeeper back-pass rule was changed in 1992, it changed everything (...), the new rule changed the possibilities for goalkeepers and added new difficulties to the position (...). At first goalkeepers were limited in trying to survive to the rule change, but now we can see that the evolution of their game has come a long way. They have become part of the game and are more important than before in the teams (...). For example, now we look at Manchester City and Ederson is almost more of an outfield player than a traditional goalkeeper.

---

88 The Coaches' Voice en español (22nd July, 2019). Clase Magistral: Juan Carlos Unzué. The role of the goalkeeper at Barcelona, from Cruyff to Luis Enrique. *El rol del portero en el Barcelona, desde Cruyff a Luis Enrique.* Extracted from: **https://www. youtube.com/watch?v=mYD15XrztDQ&feature=emb_title**

For me the change started at Ajax, between the late sixties and early seventies, because the team wanted to play a lot of time in the opposition half. When I was with Cruyff in Amsterdam we wanted to play that way and we needed goalkeepers with specific characteristics. Goalkeepers who were very good at anticipating balls that the opposition could send deep, and who could also participate as an outfield player. The change in the back-pass rule benefited this type of goalkeeper a lot, because until then it was not a very common profile. Oliver Kahn, Peter Schmeichel or Andoni Zubizarreta were very different goalkeepers to those of today".

The new regulations created a new need, from which a new type of goalkeeper began to be moulded, a goalkeeper who was required to possess virtues that were once secondary, if not outright ornamental. As centre-backs could no longer rely on them when the opposition tried to win the ball back, the usefulness of pressing forward grew, and with it the need for goalkeepers to play an effective role in securing possession and not compromising control of the ball. It is true that even before the back-pass rule, football, especially in Latin America, had seen a number of goalkeepers with a taste for playing the ball with their feet, but it was not until after 1992 that this attribute began to define the requirements of the position. The goalkeeper's footwork then began the path that would lead to it no longer being optional. It became as important and valued as other characteristics that had hitherto been much more highly valued.

"The reality is that before the rule change this type of goalkeepers were not among the best in the world, because at that time to be a good goalkeeper the important thing was the defensive aspect. The goalkeeper had to stop shots, clear side crosses and all these things. But it's interesting because with the change of the rule and the evolution of the needs of the goalkeeping position, we have seen how the level of South American or Southern European goalkeepers has increased," says Frans Hoek on the impact of goalkeepers' footwork before the transfer rule.

Santi Cañizares takes a similar approach: "I don't know if it was very productive. It shouldn't have been if only they did it. Nobody dared to do that, nor was it highly valued (...). As time went on, after the ball could no longer be played with the hand, things were different. José Molina was one of those goalkeepers who liked to play football and had a good command of the ball, and the rule was great for him because it boosted him, as at that time nobody dared to have a bit of a break or pause with the ball. The change was very good for him. Molina was effective for Atlético de Madrid, because he gave much more sense to the balls that came to his feet".

That is why Juan Carlos Unzué recalls how, despite Johan Cruyff's fondness for his goalkeepers being able to play the ball with their feet, the moments when the game required them to do so were few and far between, so that their functions as goalkeeper-player were often more aimed at positioning themselves outside the box, covering behind a very advanced defensive line, than at effectively creating advantages by intervening with their feet on the ball"[88].

For the former goalkeeper, the turning point that appears to be the trigger for the accelerated process that goalkeepers have undergone in relation to playing with their feet can be found in 2008, with the arrival of Pep Guardiola to the FC Barcelona bench: "In 2008, the feeling began to develop that we needed the goalkeeper more and more to create that first superiority (...). The first evolution was

---

89 *Ecos del balón* (13th December, 2017). A midfielder's view. *La mirada de un mediocentro* | Xabi Alonso. Recuperado de: **https://www.youtube.com/watch?v=3Ee-BHboRRkE**

marked a little by the idea of Johan Cruyff and the back-pass rule, but it really increased, both in difficulty and volume, for me clearly, from 2008 when Pep arrived".

Pep Guardiola arrived to the FC Barcelona bench with a clear idea of how he wanted his team to play, an idea that began by giving great importance to the way in which the play was constructed from the back so that the action would reach each of the following steps. That together with the ball, each player would give his team-mate a more favourable context to develop his play, thus forming a sort of footballing cataract that would reach the final metres with such force that it would be unstoppable.

Understanding that the best way to stop it was to confront it before it accumulated an excessive number of advantages, there were several opponents who articulated responses increasingly linked to forward pressure, seeking to nip in the bud the winning performance of that team and, above all, of those who henceforth drank from their idea without the degree of perfection with which Piqué, Márquez, Dani Alves, Busquets, Xavi, Iniesta and company managed to shine.

In this context of increasingly effective forward pressure, capable of taking the breath away from the men in charge of getting the game going, many teams have sought and found in their goalkeepers an oxygen tank. One more effective player, initially freed from the harassment of the opposition, and trained to decide and analyse the game like any other player on the pitch. An ace up his sleeve with which to fight the battle of the opening up of play with an extra piece, who, unattended by his opponent, has the capacity to act on the game with an impact as equivalent as possible to that of his teammates. As a consequence, assuming that the opponent is not going to take his goalkeeper out of the goal to act as an extra defender, to distinguish the goalkeeper as the eleventh attacker is to start with a numerical superiority that is always desired.

The 2015 match between FC Barcelona, coached by Luis Enrique, and Bayern Munich, coached by Pep Guardiola, at the Camp Nou, could well serve as a summary of the above. On that day, the German side tried to deactivate the Barça machine by pressing forward, with each Bavarian player being assigned to mark a local player. It was a ten-against-ten battle fought in pairs, with only goalkeepers Marc-André ter Stegen and Manuel Neuer left out. However, it was precisely the freedom given to the Barcelona goalkeeper that thwarted the visitors' intentions, as Xabi Alonso, who played as Guardiola's midfielder in the Bayern engine room that day, would later recount: "The approach was: the three up front are very good, so we have to do everything we can to stop them getting the ball. Not Neymar, not Suárez, not Messi. And the way to stop them getting the ball was to press as hard as possible from the top. The only player who could be free was Ter Stegen (...) and he was the one who complicated everything for us. He started to play long passes. Not long balls, but long passes to Luis Suárez"[89].

The goalkeeper emancipated from the three posts and became involved in the construction of the game in order to make use of the relief denied to the rest of his team-mates, and also emancipated as the origin of a new question: if the goalkeeper with the ball is one more, should he be pressured as the rest of them are? The answer to the question was initially in the affirmative, with most teams opting to throw themselves on the goalkeeper and look for a recovery which, as the last man, could prove lethal. However, especially against goalkeepers who are more technically accurate and more lucid in their interpretation of the game, coming to their defence often means releasing a team-mate and setting him up as a pass receiver.

---

90 Ballús, Pol (2018). Ederson Moraes, o jugar con Koeman de portero. *Sport*.

"The player who goes out to press the goalkeeper is the one who shows you the way", Unzué often comments, paraphrasing Luis Enrique, noting that in order to go out to press the goalkeeper, the opponent will have had to free up another player. That player then becomes the target for the ball, either with a direct pass or after the intervention of another team-mate.

"When I as a coach have gone up against teams that want to play short, as you know what the goalkeeper generates, when you are defending you don't want them to take advantage of that. For me it was key when and how we jumped or pressed the goalkeeper (...). As a coach who likes to come out from the back, deep down I know that what he is trying to provoke is that they jump at him (...). You have to be very careful how you jump at the goalkeeper. You can't just jump at him in any way. You can't just jump at him in any way, especially head-on.

It is not surprising, therefore, that in certain situations, and despite the skill of goalkeepers playing the ball with their feet, several teams design forward pressures that prioritise keeping the marking on any possible receiver of the goalkeeper's passes, rather than trying to snatch the ball from the goalkeeper or to condition him for a bad shot. Stifle the goalkeeper even when he has the ball at his feet.

As if it were a game of chess in which the movements of the two players are linked, the latest evolution of the goalkeepers at the start of the play has to do with this freedom that some of them are granted by their opponents in exchange for not unprotecting other areas of the pitch. A commitment to long service such as that often embraced by Manchester City thanks to the cannon Ederson sports on his left leg, distinguishing the goalkeeper as a sort of quarterback throwing on the run into space from the far side. "It's like playing with Koeman in goal"[90], said Burnley

91 LaTdT (2020). Let's talk about football. *Parlem de Futbol.* Corporació Catalana de Mitjans Audiovisuals.

boss Sean Dyche after his side faced Guardiola's side in a match in which the City goalkeeper completed more passes than any Claret player.

The other path that many teams have taken is to distinguish their goalkeeper as an outfield player, not only in terms of his involvement in playmaking, but also in terms of his positioning on the pitch when it takes place. "I think the next evolution of football will come when the goalkeeper is involved in attacking play. The coach who has the courage to do that will be the one who will be able to attack better," Guardiola acknowledged in an interview with Catalan tv station Televisió de Catalunya, insisting on how placing the goalkeeper outside the box, occupying the theoretical position of an outfield player, allowed the coach to gain an effective upper hand"[91].

In this way, with the goalkeeper taking the spot of one of his team-mates and using his independence with the ball at his feet, the team can have one more player to direct the pass to: "When it comes to playing the ball out," Guardiola continues, "you say: no problem, the more players I have down here, the easier it is. But then you don't have them in the top attacking third. Once you've come out with the ball, you no longer have superiority. What you do down there, you do it to have superiority in more forward areas with the aim of doing damage. If you're dropping players, it's all very well but then you don't have people up top. You play the ball out so that when they receive it your inside players have superiority with the striker, with the other inside player, with the winger, with the full-back furthest from you... with whoever. So, to achieve this, to not drop forward and to make it easier, the goalkeeper will help you".

Whether occupying the space of a centre-back or forming a three-man front line that does not require the full-backs

92 Benedetti, Ignacio (2018). Interview with Jon Pascua Ibarrola. *The Tactical Room* #44.

or any of the midfielders to leave their position, the trend that is beginning to sweep through football is for goalkeepers to play outside the box in positions that were not theirs to play in the past. The goalkeeper-player or sweeper-keeper is not only a goalkeeper because of his ability and value playing the ball with his feet, but also because of the areas of the pitch from which he does so.

A decade after the elaborate backline inspired by Pep Guardiola's team models encouraged forward pressing as a response and emphasised the need for goalkeepers involved with the ball at the start of the play, it is not unusual to find goalkeepers such as Ederson Moraes, Marc-André ter Stegen, Manuel Neuer, André Onana, Claudio Bravo, Péter Gulácsi or Julian Pollersbeck intervening outside the box in their teams' attacks. Jon Pascua Ibarrola guessed as much in 2018, in the pages of *The Tactical Room*: "I think the future lies in a three-player start with the goalkeeper splitting. Let me explain: it's like the start of many teams, playing with three centre-backs, or with two and the midfielder gets in, but I imagine that start with the goalkeeper fifteen metres out of the box. Like a football player in total attack"[92].

As well as allowing teammates to move to other areas of the pitch, for example, by adding passing options behind the pressure, the occupation of advanced areas by the goalkeeper has also been used as a way of challenging the freedom that the opponent gives them when trying to maintain man-to-man match-ups with the rest of the players. As a sort of camouflaged lure of easy prey, it encourages opponents to look for the steal or force their mistake, allowing the team that enjoys possession to open up a way forward:

"The handicap I see to those kinds of goalkeeper situations outside the box, to be able to do them as a player, is

---

93 LaTdT (2020). "Let's talk about football". *Parlem de Futbol*. Corporació Catalana de Mitjans Audiovisuals.

the difficulty that outside the box it is for the goalkeeper to drive, split and pass a ball when the opponent doesn't press you," Unzué comments. "Because when an opponent doesn't press you have to go and provoke him. You have to drive towards him so that he makes a decision and so that the pass you make offers a greater advantage to the player who is going to receive it (...). What it does do is that, against teams that are waiting in a medium backline, with that positioning of the goalkeeper what you end up doing is provoking them to be a bit braver and in the end one of them dares to go and put you under pressure".

Due to the risk that is taken in the event of a possible loss of the ball in the build-up phase, with the goalkeeper far from the goal and, therefore, in an unfavourable situation to resolve the danger that the opponent may generate if he manages to recover the ball, a fundamental aspect when carrying out these actions is the management and coexistence with their risks and limitations. You can't use the goalkeeper every time like you use the centre-backs," Guardiola continued in his explanation, "because if you lose it they score a goal from midfield. You have to do it in the first action or in the second, but after that the goalkeeper has to go back in case there is a potential loss of the ball"[93].

"You have to know how to measure the risk," says Hoek: "When you do this, one very important thing is to see how far the goalkeeper can go, because if he goes all the way to midfield, the goal is empty (...). Sometimes there are goalkeepers who are too far back and that is not necessary, but there are also goalkeepers who are too far forward". Perhaps because of this, in contexts where the team loses the ball in the build-up phase with the goalkeeper too

94 Olmeda, Miguel (2017). "We are close to winning the Europa League". "*Nos vemos cerca de ganar la Europa League*". *El Comercio*.

far from the goals, some goalkeepers begin to prioritise a response that is more oriented towards defending the ball, staying out of the box like an outfield player, than running backwards because the distance does not allow them to get there in time. Responding with pressure after a loss to try to prevent the shot, given the difficulty of stopping it if the opponent has the chance to take it.

André Onana, Ajax goalkeeper, is one of those who has sometimes responded in this way to a difficult situation outside the box: "I try to be a modern goalkeeper, not the typical one who stays under the sticks and just stops. I try to help my team in many aspects: footwork, coming off the ball, being forward off my line and cutting aerial balls. But above all, I try to transmit confidence, which is what my team needs. To give them the confidence that they can play with me, that they always know I am there (...). At a club like Ajax, which always likes to have the ball, the goalkeeper has to do that. The coach asks me to do it. He says to me: 'Onana, you take your chances. If you miss, it's my fault. If I have to miss a thousand times, I'll do it again until I get it right[94].

Goalkeeping is a position that has a close and lasting relationship with error. Not because he misses more than other players, but because, given his usual positioning as the last man in the team, it is easier for him to make a mistake in the end. "Over the years I've learned to appreciate the risk involved in every situation," Ter Stegen told Líbero magazine in an interview[95]. If behind a midfielder's mistake the defence waits as a safety net, and behind the backline the goalkeeper as a last cushion, behind the goalkeeper's back there is only the goal line as a metaphor for the abyss. His is, therefore, a personality carved out of an exposed and ungrateful ultimate responsibility,

---

95 Barcala, Diego (2019). Ciudadano Ter Stegen: "At Barcelona I feel at home". *"En Barcelona me siento en casa"*. Revista *Líbero*.

an often painful but ultimately hardening training, which in many cases has also helped him to take on the task of playing beyond his known domain, to risk a dishonourable mistake and, in spite of all this, not to stray from the path.

The 2011-2012 season was Pep Guardiola's last at FC Barcelona, and the first in which his team would ultimately fail to win the league title. An almost immaculate start by José Mourinho's Madrid, coupled with a few slip-ups by the Catalan giants, meant that Los Blancos had a six-point gap to their opponents before the first clásico of the season was played at the Santiago Bernabéu on matchday 16. With more than a round still to play and many points still to be shared, leaving Madrid's stadium with a nine-point deficit was not definitive, but given the precedent of the two previous seasons and the very high scores achieved by the two teams in those games, the match took on the tinge of a final in the event of a home victory. In the first minute of the game, an error in the pass by Víctor Valdés gave the ball to Di María, as a prelude to an early goal by Karim Benzema.

But neither Víctor nor Barça changed their intentions regarding the short pass. Nor about the importance of the Catalan goalkeeper in it. The defence continued to rely on their goalkeeper, and he continued to play his part in the game as if the Real Madrid goal had not existed. Then came goals from Alexis Sánchez, Xavi Hernández and Cesc Fàbregas, turning the scoreline around and sealing a victory that started with a bang and allowed Guardiola's side to close in on the league leaders. It was a reaction that Pep explained in the post-match press conference through his goalkeeper: "The perfect image of how the team responded is that Víctor Valdés, after the goal, kept playing the ball. I congratulated him in front of everyone because it is a demonstration of his strength and the strength of this team. Another goalkeeper would have started to play the ball long (...). I'd rather he lost this ball, I'd rather he lost

another one, but most of the time we're still giving continuity to the game from the back".

Trained under the stylistic umbrella of La Masia, the residence where the young talents of FC Barcelona's youth teams are taught, from a very young age Víctor Valdés declared himself an admirer of Oliver Kahn and Santi Cañizares, whom he never hesitated to point out as his great references in goal. Both of them, like him, loved to block the ball rather than clear it, neither of them had been characterised by a particularly strong game with their feet, but both had a strong personality and character that a goalkeeper who was so exposed would need. "You asked me earlier what goalkeepers like Valdés or Kasper Schmeichel could see in me. I think on the one hand it's the blocking and on the other hand it's the personality. For me the most important thing for a goalkeeper is personality. The goalkeeper has to be a leader," says Cañizares.

Kahn was also a role model for Ter Stegen, despite the differences in style between the two. "Our style is different, but I would look up to him for his mentality"[96], admitted the FC Barcelona goalkeeper. "I didn't like him for his game but more for his character and mentality to always want to win and always be 100% motivated in any match. And this is why he is one of my idols. He knew how to do that and motivate his team. He was a leader and I liked that"[97].

Nowadays, the normality with which younger goalkeepers incorporate the particularities of the role of goalkeeper has also been boosted and benefited by the proximity of references as a mirror. I wanted to be like Arkonada," says Unzué, "and nowadays young goalkeepers want to be like

---

96 Revista *Panenka* (2018). Ter Stegen: "I wouldn't be here if I didn't know how to play with my feet". "*No estaría aquí si no supiera jugar con los pies*". *Panenka*.

97 Barcala, Diego (2019). Ciudadano Ter Stegen: "At Barcelona I feel at home". "*En Barcelona me siento en casa*". Revista *Líbero*.

Ter Stegen, like Ederson, like Neuer, like Oblak too... they want to be like their idols. That's why, whether their coach asks them to or not, they are already mentally prepared to play that game".

A reality that Cañizares illustrates from his experience with his son, also a goalkeeper: "I give you the example of my son, and therefore we are talking about two completely different generations. Sometimes I can't go to watch his games and then he tells me: 'I had a great game today'. And when I ask him what he did, he says: 'Well, I didn't get a lot of shots, only once from outside the box, but I played the ball 20 times with my right foot, six or seven times with my left and I did it well'. Is that a great game? Of course, for him it is.

However, despite his absolute importance, it is not only in terms of footwork that the role of the goalkeeper has changed in recent years. The desire of many teams to press their opponents from the back, and the consequent use and enjoyment of very advanced defensive lines, has pushed goalkeepers to establish a very advanced position on the pitch. When their team sets up close to the opposition goal, they position themselves outside the box in such a way that they can influence the space behind their defenders. In the manner of the old sweeper, they are bodyguards in charge of covering the back of the centre-backs, coming out to cut out the passes that the opposition can filter behind the defence, if not directly discouraging them by their mere presence.

Víctor Valdés explains: "With Guardiola my defensive line always went to midfield, and there were usually 30 or 40 metres that I had to defend like another defender. And that was complicated. My position had to be much more advanced than that of another goalkeeper"[98].

---

98 Marlon Becerra Entrevista (2015). Interview with Víctor Valdés. TV Colombia (RCN Internacional).

"All modern keepers like Ter Stegen or De Gea, are keepers who do not remain under the sticks", describes André Onana [99], regarding the conduct of the goalkeeper that is very widespread, with the priority being to anticipate the chance of danger before having to deal with it. It is, therefore, a use of the goalkeeper that does not focus on the save but on how to avoid it: "People can get excited about that save, because it is impressive, but I think about what to do before a save, which for me is the last resort"[100].

It was along these lines that Juan Carlos Unzué decided to work with Víctor Valdés when they both worked together for Frank Rijkaard's Barça: "I used to say to Víctor: 'You probably have the idea that you've got to where you are because of what you've saved. (...) But let me ask you a question: what do you prefer in the end: that you get eight or ten shots every game and, therefore, the chance of the opposition scoring is greater, or that you only get three, four or five shots on goal? Obviously, you're going to get fewer shots because you're going to get fewer goals that way. Well, by playing this way you're going to get it".

On the 30th July 2014, the German national team met Algeria in the last 16 of the FIFA World Cup. Joachim Löw's men won in extra time with goals from André Schürrle and Mesut Özil, but the name of the game was their goalkeeper. Beyond his effectiveness in front of goal, what impressed the world about Manuel Neuer's performance was the volume and accuracy of his involvement away from goal. On 21 occasions he touched the ball out of the box (37% of his total appearances in the match)[101], and in as many as 17 of them he did so by anticipating a pass

---

99 Ramiro, Emmanuel (2018). Interview with André Onana. *The Tactical Room #41.*

100 Herrera De La Fuente, Claudio (2020). Frans Hoek, legendary Dutch goalkeeper coach: "I don't know what happened with Bravo in the Premier League". *ícono holandés en la preparación de goleros: "No sé qué pasó con Bravo en la Premier League".* *El Mercurio* newspaper.

101 Marcet. Intelligent Football: How the goalkeeper has become a sweeper. *Cómo el portero se convirtió en líbero.* Extracted from: **https://marcetfootball.com/es/como-el-portero-se-convirtio-en-libero/**

from an Algerian player behind the German defence[102]. He acted as a sweeper-keeper, protecting the metres Germany conceded between the defence and his own goal in order to keep the block as close together and as far forward as possible. Moving away from the save, he stepped up to prevent a dangerous chance. "Manu is always focused; he is never distracted. He's playing the game even if he's not involved. He's playing every second of every minute," said Guardiola a few months later, after Bayern Munich's 2-0 win over Rudi Garcia's AS Roma in the UEFA Champions League[103].

"If I'm off my line, it's to help. It's not for me, it's for the team", explained his countryman Ter Stegen when journalist Jordi Quixano asked him on the pages of newspaper El País if he didn't mind playing so far away from his goal-line[104].

Despite the greater difficulty and exposure goalkeepers have had in terms of their importance in attacking play, both in terms of footwork and positioning outside the box, their constant participation and involvement while the team has the ball has also served to facilitate their connection with what is happening during matches. Far from the figure who in the past was reserved to a very limited number of appearances and therefore had greater difficulty in staying mentally activated when he had to respond to them to the best of his ability, today's goalkeeper is a goalkeeper whose value in matches is uninterrupted and with a continuity that makes no distinction between the different phases of the game. The modern goalkeeper plays when his team is attacking and when the opposition is attacking. When the ball is close to his goal and when

---

102 Eurosport (2014). Eurosport: Alemania pone en práctica una enseñanza de Guardiola. Recuperado de: https://www.eurosport.es/futbol/mundial/2014/alemania-pone-en-practica-una-ensenanza-de-guardiola_sto4310396/story.shtml

103 Perarnau, Martí (2016). *Pep Guardiola. La metamorfosis*. Barcelona, España: Editorial Córner.

104 Quixano, Jordi (2017). Ter Stegen: "I don't take fewer risks, but I calculate them better". *"No asumo menos riesgos sino que los calculo mejor"*. El País.

it is far away. He never disconnects from the game. He is not allowed to do so.

This is how Juan Carlos Unzué sees it when he analyses how "even though the demands are greater now, I think that all this has helped the goalkeeper to be more attentive to the game in a natural way. It doesn't happen like years ago when there were goalkeepers who were in their own little area and maybe appeared three times in a game. It was more complicated to be at one hundred per cent of your mental and physical capacities".

For Cañizares, however, there is a relevant difference in the type of activation that a goalkeeper finds when he touches the ball with his feet compared to when he touches it with his hands: "Indeed, making contact with the ball is always pleasant in a match, but they are such different actions mechanically that they have nothing to do with each other. A goalkeeper is still going to be cold if he doesn't have the opportunity to play with his hand. For the activity in general, yes, having participation with the foot and being active can help, but mechanically they are such different actions that what a goalkeeper is looking for is to block two or three balls either in side crosses or shots on goal".

In parallel to the possible advantage the goalkeeper finds in his volume of participation, in terms of easier activation, Frans Hoek points to the difficulty and importance goalkeeper positioning has gained: "For me now positioning is the most important thing. The game is a positional game, also for the goalkeeper (...). Today it is more difficult because the goalkeeper moves every time the ball moves. Every time the ball moves the goalkeeper's situation changes, and to be prepared in every situation you have to move according to the movement of the ball. Today goalkeepers run between one or two kilometres more per game (...) Before, the goalkeeper would wait under the posts, react when a ball was kicked to him and that was it. That has changed incredibly. Not surprisingly, David De

Gea, who worked with Hoek for two seasons at Manchester United, admits that positioning is the area in which he has made the most progress thanks to the Dutch coach[105].

The proliferation of teams that opt to place their defensive line away from their own goal has not only had an impact on the type of positioning that is often required of goalkeepers in attack, but also on the type of actions they must respond to in defence. It has increased the likelihood of goalkeepers having to face one-on-one situations against the striker, to the point that Víctor Valdés did not hesitate to mention it when asked about the fundamental characteristic that the club should look for in his replacement when he announced his departure from Barcelona: "I have always thought that the Barça goalkeeper has to be the best in one-on-one situations. Statistics say that the goalkeeper will come up with 25-30 one-on-ones that will decide games"[106].

"In the old days, the defences were much further back," Cañizares reflects. "In the seventies or eighties, especially the seventies, goalkeepers hardly ever left the penalty area. Like Sepp Maier, for example. Now defenders defend much higher up, trying to narrow the field, to reduce the spaces, and they make the goalkeeper stand on the edge or outside the box, having to intervene on long balls behind the defenders. That started to exist in my time, and I had to learn to do that job. Right now, a Barcelona goalkeeper, for example, has a lot of one-on-ones during the year, and as Valdés, who is a wise man in goal, says, they need to respond in this type of situation. If we go back to other times, one-on-one situations were absolutely sporadic, it's something to do with the position of the defence".

---

105 Santomé, Sergio (2014). MarcadorInt: Cómo ha cambiado De Gea dentro y fuera del campo. Recuperado de: https://www.marcadorint.com/premier-league/como-ha-cambiado-de-gea-dentro-y-fuera-del-campo/
106 *El correo gallego* (2013). Valdés reiterates his decision as "irrevocable" on leaving FC Barcelona. *El correo gallego*.

As a result, just as the need for the goalkeeper to intervene more and better with his feet has made his game evolve, so too has having to adapt to the increase in one-on-one situations by improving his response to them. "In one-on-one situations, positioning, patience and technique are very important," explains Hoek, "when I was a goalkeeper, it was normal that when the striker faced you in one-on-one situations, you went to the ground too quickly. Aspects in many cases imported from Latin American goalkeepers that have allowed goalkeepers to be more effective in preventing goals, avoiding dribbles by strikers and many of the penalties and sending offs that all too often ended in such situations in the past.

So, while the final saves are still similar to what they used to be, much of what happens before they happen has changed. Along with the increase in hand-to-hand actions, for example, there has developed a trend of goalkeepers and coaches favouring the benefits of tackling closer to the goal line than was once considered appropriate, both in frontal and lateral actions.

Traditionally the best position for the goalkeeper to respond to a shot was slightly in front of the goal line to eat up space for the shot and to be able to clear the ball without the danger that if the rebound went a little backwards it might find its way into the goal. Recently, however, there has been a growing tendency for some goalkeepers to prefer to gain reaction time by delaying their position in front of the striker's shot. I've been more of a space-saving type," says Unzué, "but like everything else, it depends on the characteristics of your goalkeeper. You can have a goalkeeper who is taller, less dynamic, less reactive, and maybe it's better for him to be two metres further back because even if he has to cover a little more space, his wingspan will compensate for it".

"As in everything, there is virtue in the middle ground," says Cañizares. "Stopping on the line gives you more reaction time, it's true. But it is more difficult to clear a ball because your clearance has to be at least parallel to your body (...). If you're on the line you have more reaction time, but you cover fewer goals, and the blocks are less grateful because they have to be very strong (...). If you play a bit further forward you are reducing your shooting angle. You have less ability to react, but if you touch the ball, any blocked shot, even if it's deflected backwards, gets out of the goal because you're so far forward".

Probably the area where the goalkeepers' final response to the striker's shot has changed the most is in the predominance of clearing over blocking. The current characteristics of the balls and pitches, as well as the ability of opponents to hit them, have led goalkeepers to increasingly prioritise a good clearance technique that not only avoids a goal but also minimises the chances of a second chance, rather than an attempt to block the ball which, due to the difficulties involved, opens the door to an incomplete action that makes things easier for the striker in the second instance. To achieve the initiative in the action, from the dominance of the deflection. "My memory is that the aerial balls I used to catch in my time were much more pumped balls and you had more time to be able to go out and get them (...), now they are balls that make more tin, partly because of the speed and partly because of the materials they use", comments Juan Carlos Unzué, giving context to a vision of the preparation of goalkeepers in which the time invested in improving clearances is greater than the time spent on blocking: "You have to work in relation to the type of situations that are going to occur. Then, if for the evolution of football or for whatever reasons you feel that there is a lot of difficulty in blocking, you have to give less time. However you have to improve the type of clearing you do. Possibly what I would do is spend a lot of time working on the quality of those clearances. On the quality of that clearance, because that kind of situation is going to happen a lot more than the two or three times, you're going to be able to block a ball during the game".

In the same way that the new responsibilities of goal-keepers have formally modified the type of preparation for goalkeepers, for example by increasing the amount of time they spend training with their teammates, their new reality has also changed the content of their specific work. Spending more time improving aspects such as footwork or deflecting shots means, at the same time, taking time away from other tasks. This is how Santi Cañizares illustrates it: "If we are using a lot more time in the goalkeeper's training work for the game with the feet (...) we are taking it away from somewhere. I remember that with Miguel Ángel at Real Madrid, who was my goalkeeping coach at youth level, or with José Manuel Ochotorena, who was the best goalkeeping coach I've ever had, we worked for hours and hours on blocking (...). In the end they are hours of work, and if we are using them to work on some things that are also important, there are others that we are working on less. And that is noticeable. We are reaping the rewards of our work with the feet, there is no doubt about it, but if we are cutting time on training other things, we won't be able to improve them".

That's why Frans Hoek emphasises training during the formative stages: "It's very important that in grassroots football we work a lot on basic situations. In the younger age categories the balls are not as fast and it's a good time to practise blocking. When they are older, the strikers' shots are stronger and the ball goes faster," says the Dutch coach, who years ago, working with FC Barcelona's youth goalkeepers, came across a special pair of goalkeepers. "I've always been very interested in junior and youth grassroots football, and when I came to Barça I wanted to know what the youth goalkeepers were like. From time to time I worked with them, and in the case of Reina and Valdés it was very easy to see their talent. Their talent wasn't normal (...). I remember saying to Van Gaal: 'Louis, in the youth system I've seen two goalkeepers who are 16 years old but who look like they're already 18 or 19.

They need to move up a category, because the team they are in is too small for them'. A year later they were already training with the first team. It was harder for them because they were training with the best players in the world and every shot was a goal. They had never taken those shots before, but in time that was going to make them improve. And they did.

The early talent that Hoek spotted in Victor Valdes was, for a long time, a kind of punishment for the Catalan goal-keeper. A gift that chained him to a destiny he did not want for himself: "My dream was to be a player"[107]. Victor did not want to be a goalkeeper. Sometimes he even couldn't bear to be one. Like when, at the age of eleven, he decided to leave La Masía and put his career in goal on hold. Victor was pained by the loneliness of the goal and the distance that condemned him to watch from too far away how the rest of his teammates played together. That is why Victor, despite accepting his destiny as a goalkeeper, took it in his own way. Being a goalkeeper would not deprive him of being just another footballer. The gloves would not be shackles, but the safeguard to be a footballer with privileges. To be as much a player as the rest and as an extra, just as an extra, to be able to touch the ball with his hands inside his own area. To be unique by playing like everyone else.

---

107 *Informe Robinson* (2011). "Víctor Valdés". Canal +

CHAPTER 4

THE RIGHTS OF THE FULL-BACKS

> "In today's football, I have no doubt that the most important are the full-backs. They give you life"[108]
>
> DIEGO PABLO SIMEONE

Something is not right. Something is not going to plan. The game is yet to start, but Guardiola and Tito Vilanova agitate on the bench. The first match-up between Pep's Barça and Mourinho's Madrid is about to start, a few months after Inter Milan under the Portuguese manager eliminated the Blaugrana out of the Champions League, and both the Catalan coach and his assistant have detected something they need to communicate to their players: Cristiano Ronaldo and Ángel Di María are starting the match on the wings and have switched sides. The Portuguese starlet will be on the right and the Argentine on the left, which clashes with one of the adjustments Guardiola

---

108 *FOX Sports Sur* (2019). *90 Minutos.* Interview with Diego *Cholo* Simeone.

has prepared for the clash. Pep wanted Carles Puyol to be the centre-back closest to Real Madrid's number seven. This is why Carles was switched to the right of Gerard Piqué and not to his left, as is more common, and this is why instructions to the centre pairing from the bench are for them to return to their original positions. Puyol must play close to Cristiano Ronaldo to help his full-back in defence without having the need for Piqué to cover out wide. The instruction by Guardiola and Vilanova is given right on time, the defenders comply with the order and one of the happiest and most brilliant matches that the Camp Nou has ever seen in the club's history began. A 5-0 win to remember.

Dani Alves was the only player who did not move from his position, as a result of this merry-go-round of positions between Madrid's forwards and Barça's centre-backs. In Pep Guardiola's side, the Brazilian was more than a wing-back. His attacking impact and the versatility with which he could express it meant he was a wildcard for the team that the coach could use in different ways depending on his strategy at any given moment. A clear-sighted initiator from the back, a fourth midfielder bursting into the wide area by surprise or the player in charge of occupying the right flank on his own so that the team could gain personnel in other areas of the pitch. A full-back, an inside player and a winger, all in the body of a unique player. Of a very unique player.

For the opposition, facing him meant facing all three, forcing them to take precautions that, as a rule, the other full-backs did not require. Mourinho had had to adapt to this in the aforementioned tie between Barça and Inter Milan that paved the way for the Nerazzurri's treble. Against a different Culé side, which had Ibrahimović up front and in which Messi often started from the right, but in which, equally, Dani Alves assumed an almost absolute offensive relevance. By joining the attack, the full-back allowed Leo to get close to the box without his opponents being able to disengage from Barcelona's right flank. In that double pairing duel, first Goran Pandev and then Cristian Chivu were in charge of defending the Brazilian full-back. They were embedded in midfield if Alves did so or dressed as full-backs if Dani had to be chased into a winger's position.

Months later, on the eve of the first clásico at the Camp Nou, Mourinho chose Ángel Di María to fulfil the same mission. The Argentinian was to shadow Dani Alves on Madrid's left flank, but as his usual position in the Madrid set-up was on the right, he was to swap places with Cristiano Ronaldo. Thus the Portuguese winger, on the opposite flank to the Brazilian full-back, would be relieved of the defensive work that the latter would have demanded of him. It was the recipe that Mourinho designed to set up a specific defence against Barça's right-back without giving up the freshness of his most decisive striker, and which forced Guardiola to adjust the position of his centre-backs seconds before kick-off.

The figure of the attacking full-back embodied by Dani Alves in Guardiola's Barça is an archetype that the history of football has seen appear more or less recurrently. Despite the fact that until recently the unwritten rules of football said that the priority for a full-back should be defence and the ability to cut off the opposition's advances down the flank, so that his hypothetical offensive contribution had its place, afterwards, as an interesting and very productive addition normally considered in the background. Silvio Marzolini, Giacinto Facchetti, Carlos Alberto, Wim Suurbier, Paul Breitner, Júnior, Eric Gerets, Rafael Gordillo, Cafú, Roberto Carlos... Full-backs with different characteristics to the others, capable of making an impact near the opposition goal as if they were a winger and to open up new possibilities for coaches that were out of reach for the rest of the teams. Full-backs who could be entrusted with a role with the ball at their feet that was unattainable for other members of their species.

At Guardiola's Barcelona, Dani Alves was the quintessential representative of the breed. An ace up the coach's sleeve, which at times allowed the Catalan to bring him close to the ball as if he were just another midfielder, and at other times, he dressed up as a winger so that it was the theoretical striker who would add an extra piece of skill to the engine room. In the same lane that Xavi Hernández and Leo Messi used to play, and which between the three of them made it the safest habitat for the ball during the time they were able to share it, the Brazilian winger was a unique and exclusive advantage for the Blaugrana side. An initially individual superiority that has also become a collective superiority through the whiteboard.

Manolo Jiménez, his last coach at Sevilla, described him as "a player who from his position at right-back is capable of setting up the attacking football of an entire team, who in one-on-one play is a star and who can make any coach happy"[109]. A player with a creative impact on the attacking play and who, starting from the back and from the flank, enjoyed more space than the rest of his attacking partners, normally more constrained by the defences near the opposing area. Guardiola's Barça achieved victory through control of the ball, and, thanks to Dani Alves, they had one more piece than their opponents. A piece, moreover, very closely linked on the pitch with the team's most important player: "I used to make a pass that Guardiola doesn't like very much. I'm talking about the pass from the full-back to the winger. That pass is a false pass. For the ball to reach the winger properly, the pass has to go from the wing to the middle and from the middle to the wing. But I often gave that pass to Messi. I spoke to Guardiola and I told him: Coach, if Messi spends two minutes without touching the ball, he disconnects from the game. So as Leo has to be ready to define the play, he has to be

____

109 Morén, Albert (2016). *En un momento dado*: Dani Alves: eterno e infinito. Extracted from: https://eumd.es/2016/08/repaso-despedida-dani-alves-barca/

connected to the game. So I'm going to take care of connecting him"[110].

It is difficult to know which came first. The end of the pure winger or the end of the finishing striker. Whether the former died out when they ran out of specialists in the box to whom to pass a ball from the flank after dribbling past a pair and gaining the back line, or whether it was the latter who, with no aerial balls to be fed from the wing, adopted a more diverse brand of football. Whatever the correct order of events, the result ended up being the same: wide attackers with a tendency to appear in central areas and a preference for playing with their opposite foot - that is, left-footed on the right and right-footed on the left - and lanes delegated to the attacking weight of the full-backs.

Pablo Zabaleta, an Argentinian player who has shared a lane with attackers of all abilities throughout his career in the Argentinian, Spanish and English leagues, explains from first-hand experience the relationship between the full-back and the winger, and how the context of the full-back changes if the team-mate in front of him plays with a natural leg or with his left foot: "When you have a right-footed player in front of you, a player like Jesús Navas, who was a player who in one-on-one was very much looking to go wide and be able to cross because he had pace, you don't need to be a full-back who projects all the time, because it's important to leave it to him in the one-on-one. You can be an option so that, if he can't cross, he can play backwards and then take the play to the other side. Playing with a left-footed player, with his left-foot, it does give you the opportunity to go forward almost every time, because a left-footed player in the one-on-one is always going to look to go inside to get a shot off. A lot of time he drags the full-back inside and that's when you can come on (...) Ribéry and Robben, Barcelona at the time...

---

110 Fra, Amalia (2019). El día que Dani Alves corrigió a Guardiola para tener a Messi atento al juego. *As newspaper.*

many teams started to use the 1-4-3-3 with wingers on the left, and they needed deep full-backs to generate superiority on the flank"[111].

His compatriot Nicolás Tagliafico agrees, stressing the importance of the partnerships established between full-backs and wingers: "You have to know your team-mate. You have to know his characteristics, know what he likes and dislikes.... I've played with all kinds of players there, with very quick, agile, and skilful strikers like David Neres or Justin Kluivert. Or like Di María, who is a more vertical player... And you have to know them and know their tastes. For example, I know that Tadić can get inside and hold the ball thanks to his physicality, and that gives me the possibility that when he receives the ball, I can turn him wide. But on the other hand, with quicker wingers, I know that it's better for me to play inside to create a problem for the full-back. Make him close down a bit and then the ball, instead of going through me, goes straight to the winger to allow him one on one with more space. Di María, as well as being quick, is very vertical, so I know that when I play with him instead of doubling him on the wing, I have to offer him support. When he gets the ball, he's going to want to beat his marker either by dribbling or by speed, and if I turn him wide, I'm going to bring another defender into his space"[112].

The growing tendency to accumulate players in the centre of the pitch, the gradual disappearance of the canonical figure of the winger, and the appearance of special full-backs with an enormous impact on attacking duties, has changed the way this position is perceived. What was once an add-on, his offensive weight, is now part of the main plan. It can be said that, generally speaking, the classic characteristics of the more typically Brazilian full-back

111 *En un momento dado* (2021). Interview with Pablo Zabaleta. Extracted from: https://eumd.es/2021/04/entrevista-pablo-zabaleta/

112 *En un momento dado* (2021). Interview with Nicolás Tagliafico. Extracted from: https://eumd.es/2021/04/entrevista-nicolas-tagliafico/

have won out over the traditional Italian full-back proto-type[113]. In the same way that it is the case with goalkeepers and their ability to play the ball with their feet, or with centre-backs and their ability to bring the ball out from the back, so too in the case of full-backs, the exception has become the norm.

"In the old days, in the teams, people at the back were limited to defending very well and the attacking players were the strikers and midfielders. At the moment when there has been an evolution in football and teams have understood that by having better ball control, they would have a better chance of winning, the evolution has been that players with good technique have also been taking up positions further back", says Eusebio Sacristán.

To move into the elite, being autonomous players on the ball and capable of being important in the final metres of the pitch are no longer virtues of full-backs subordinated to a good defensive performance but have generally become the calling card of those who want to occupy the position in a top level team. Today, the full-back has turned that statement on its head. His contribution in the opposition half is the part that the team cannot do without and, on the other hand, his defensive performance allows for more nuances and a greater adaptation of the team as a whole.

Juande Ramos, who coached Dani Alves for two full seasons at Sevilla, recalls his work with the Brazilian full-back: "Dani is a player who has to be given freedom. You have to let him develop his full attacking potential because otherwise you're limiting him. If you tell him that he's a defender and not to go beyond midfield, you're losing his great virtues: stamina, and the ability to help in attacking play (...). When you have a player like Dani, who has that

---

113 Quintana, Miguel (4th May, 2020). The great evoution of the full-back. *La gran evolución del lateral* | With Alberto López. Extracted from: **https://youtu.be/-AvoQtU-GJmQ**

attacking potential, and you want to take advantage of it, there is a defensive deficiency, because his area is always left quite uncovered. Then you need other players to be on their toes to solve any problems that may arise. In our case, Christian Poulsen was the one who corrected it"[114]. Sharing the right flank with Jesús Navas, protected by the cover of Christian Poulsen and with partners in the penalty area such as Luis Fabiano or Frédéric Kanouté, during his time at Sevilla, Alves won two UEFA Cups, a Copa del Rey, a Spanish Super Cup and a European Super Cup, before continuing to add to his trophy cabinet at FC Barcelona.

Thus, if during the first decade of the 2000s most Champions League contenders had a full-back in their ranks who was more closely linked to the centre-back position than the winger, with examples such as Maldini, Abidal, Ivanović, Wes Brown, Gallas, Oleguer, Chivu, Sergio Ramos and Arbeloa, a decade later it is commong to find archetypes such as Alexander-Arnold, Alphonso Davies, Marcelo, Kimmich, Filipe Luis, Trippier, Robertson, Carvajal, Jordi Alba, Marcos Alonso, Robin Gosens, Achraf Hakimi, João Cancelo and Jesús Navas commanding the positioning. Men with a lot of attacking range and with the ability to have an effect in the opposition's half more typical of a striker. It is not in vain that several full-backs of this era have arrived at the position after having played in more advanced areas. Converting attackers into wingers so that they can play as wingers from their new position, with the same objective that Johan Cruyff discovered in the early nineties to explain the recycling of players such as Jon Andoni Goikoetxea or Sergi Barjuán: "If the full-back arrives as a winger, his winger has to play as a winger. And ours are better at attacking than theirs are at defending"[115].

---

114 *En un momento dado* (2021). Interview with Juande Ramos. Extracted from: https://eumd.es/2021/04/entrevista-juande-ramos/
115 *Informe Robinson* (2009). "Johan Cruyff". Canal +

From Amsterdam, almost half a century after Johan left Ajax for Barcelona, Tagliafico defends (and attacks) the Dutch side's left-back position. "The full-back can do a lot of things," says the Argentinian. "Nowaday, the full-back is a position that generates a lot of surprises. It also creates a lot of problems for opponents, because you start from very low down and you usually get marked by opponents who are strikers and don't usually defend very well".

"I've been up top, and they've defended me, so you learn", said Jesús Navas of his move to right-back. "I'm really enjoying that position. I like it, I have a lot of space in front of me, I like to go forward, I'm a player who likes to attack. Of course it's important to defend, but whenever I get the chance I always look forward (...). If you look at my beginnings, it helped me a lot to have Dani Alves. He was a player who went up a lot and when he did, I had his back. We swapped positions a lot. Guardiola wanted to put me at full-back because he already knew me from those years, and he didn't hesitate"[116].

Often having to play alone on the wing and, therefore, taking the place of a winger in the final metres, the full-back has had to adapt his offensive characteristics to a new playing context. "Football has evolved a lot and full-backs have to know how to move in attacking areas, that's why there are a lot of converted wingers", explains Spain international Juan Bernat in relation to the position of players who are used to playing as wingers[117].

Their role, often, is not longer to appear by surprise, running without the ball into space, taking advantage of the advanced presence of a winger who fixes the attention of the opposing defence and allows them to run down the flank with freedom to deliver a cross into the box from a

---

116 Yunta, Enrique (2019). Jesús Navas: " I eat a lot but I don't stand still". *"Como un montón, pero no paro quieto"*. *ABC newspaper.*

117 Valle, Conrado (2019). Bernat: "I fight every day at PSG to be able to play for Spain". *"Lucho cada día en el PSG para poder estar con España"*. *As newspaper.*

corner. The fact is that now, sometimes being being the only reference point on the flanks, they are being called upon to provide the attributes that were once used by the wingers to bring danger down the flank. "In one of the first talks I had with Ernesto Valverde −recalls Zabaleta− he told me that he had Andoni Iraola at Athletic Bilbao, and that with me he wanted to reproduce that type of player. A player that he could use as a full-back and that in other games he could use further forward. Ernesto wanted deep full-backs". Full-back is the position in which Zabaleta finally settled on his arrival in the Premier League as a Manchester City player: "When you play in a team that normally controls games and has quality players to win as an attacking team, as a full-back you become practically a permanent attacking player".

On the other hand, Nicolás Tagliafico has played as a full-back practically from the start ("I've played on the wing my whole career"), which gives him a panoramic view of how the position has evolved and how he himself has had to adapt his football to the new needs of the position:

"There have been a lot of changes. I think at the beginning everything was very structured, very linear (...). My position was just to go all along the line, all along the flank. Defending and, when possible, attacking (...). I had to train a lot, adapting to the different circumstances (...). If I look at what I was ten years ago and what I am now, I see that I have changed a lot. My way of seeing football and the moments. I think that's key, because you can have a lot of technique, but if you don't choose the right moments it's complicated. When you go on the offensive phase you have to think like a striker (...). When I step into the opponent's box and I'm close to the goal, I try to be another striker".

Widening the pitch at different heights, waiting for the ball on the flanks where the opposition accumulates fewer men, because as Adrián Cervera analyses, "the fact that in the last decade we have tried to generate superiority through the centre-backs had led to opponents prioritising aggressive harassment over first inside passes, so that the spaces have come to be in lateral areas"[118]. Or by extracting defenders from the centre to allow a freer flow between the centre-backs and the midfield.

 "At Ajax we always want to play from deep, and the position of the full-backs is important", Tagliafico continues. "Sometimes the opposition pressure requires us to be very low, at the height of the big box, to attract opponents (...). If they bring a lot of people to press us, it{s the perfect moment to jump lines and be able to pass directly into the offensive zone. Other times what we do is free up a lot of space for the centre-backs, playing with the full-back high up. (...) When I arrived, the centre-backs were De Ligt and De Jong, two totally attacking players. And the first thing they taught me was that when one of them got the ball, he would start to drive. Then you had to close down as a centre-back. I had to end up forming a line of three with the other full-back and the centre-back who stayed behind. That was the first few months. Then when Frenkie started to play in the middle, what he did a lot was drift out to the wing, as if he was a full-back, and then I was the one who had to stretch the pitch to create space for him".

 In this sense, the new place that full-backs occupy in the attacking approach of their teams has put a new value on attributes that in the past did not belong to them, such as dribbling. Whether it is to deal with forward pressures or to unbalance on the wing in the vicinity of the opposing penalty area, the full-back with a dribble and an overlap is a master key, and as Guardiola advocated even before starting his career as a coach, "in football, when 'dummy' beats 'dummy', the defending team is lost". It is not for nothing that Madrid's Marcelo, a real specialist in the field,

---

118 *En un momento dado* (2021). Interview with Adrián Cervera. Extracted from: https://eumd.es/2021/04/entrevista-adrian-cervera/

can be considered the most decisive left-back of the last decade in European football.

But dribbling is an increasingly rare art. This is true of those players originally more linked to dribbling, such as wingers, and it is also true of those who are favoured as a novelty. That is why, when it comes to generating attacking impact, it is common for full-backs to resort to another type of tool: "I'm not a full-back who grabs the ball and goes one-on-one with the opposing defender," Tagliafico explains. "I'm a type of player who needs a more group game in which I try to generate a combination to get to the back line and send in the cross, or to combine by getting inside... I always need a team-mate to be close to me to be able to build these connections and these 2-v-1. And generally when I play with a winger, having communication, we can generate a lot of problems for the opposing full-back. If one stays open and the other closes down, you end up making the pitch too big for him and he doesn't know which of the two to defend".

Alexander-Arnold's infinite striking ability[119], Jordi Alba's link-up play with Leo Messi at Barcelona, Davies' explosiveness at Bayern Munich and Kimmich's ability to play associatively when his coaches choose to place him on the wing are examples of a wide and diverse palette of colours.

Recently, however, several teams are exploiting the possibility of hurting their opponents by taking advantage of the attacking role they entrust to their full-backs. This is because, despite being transformed into wingers for many minutes of the game, they still retain the responsibility of defensively occupying the space on either side of the backline. The full-back is asked to attack as high up the pitch as possible, but at the same time, he has to get down

---

119 Martínez, Tomàs (2018). Marcadorint: The reconversion of Trent Alexander-Arnold to succeed at the club of his life. Extracted from: **https://www.marcadorint.com/ champions-league/trent-alexander-arnold-lateral-derecho-liverpool-reconversion/**

low before the opponent when the ball changes possession.

Pablo Maffeo, a full-back trained in the youth ranks with Espanyol and who, despite his young age, already has experience with Manchester City, Girona, Stuttgart and Huesca explains: "Nowadays a full-back has to be up and down. He needs to have a lot of physicality and a lot of finishing. (...) When you arrive tired and at a lot of speed, you have to take it easy with the last touch, because sometimes you go so fast that it is difficult to control the strength or the strike of the ball"[120].

This is an issue underlined in recent times by the rise of forward pressing, a trend that has become the norm. First of all, it requires the full-backs to get forward from very early on in the game in order to fix the team's width and prevent the opposition from concentrating their pressure on the ball. The full-back, in attack, lives far away from the centre-backs of his own team, often without the figure of a team-mate in between to act as a rest in the middle. In the new football, when the ball is lost, the players close to the ball have the task of defending forward, of pressing on the start of the opponent's play and of reducing the spaces created near the action as much as possible. Forwards, inside forwards and even midfielders, rather than running backwards, must run forwards. All of them as one. There are no available pieces, detached from the action, to be given up in the pressure in exchange for using them to provide cover on the wing.

It is against this backdrop that some of the latest variations on the offensive role of the full-backs make sense. The proliferation of schemes with three centre-backs and two full-backs makes sense. Maffeo was the protagonist of one of the most characteristic of Spanish football in recent years: Pablo Machín's Girona. "The advantage of

---

120 *En un momento dado* (2021). Interview with Pablo Maffeo. Extracted from: https://eumd.es/2021/04/entrevista-pablo-maffeo/

playing with three centre-backs is that as a winger you go forward knowing that you are covered (...). I feel comfortable both ways. I've been lucky enough to have teammates who were more inclined to get inside, to play, to link up and let me play a bit more on the wing, and that's perfect for me. Playing with three central defenders I feel very comfortable because as a winger I can get more (...). The experience with Machín, with whom I was playing for a long time in this position, I believe helped me to improve offensively".

Also the increasingly widespread use of the figure of the full-back-midfielder. These are full-backs that keep their value intact on the ball and their absolute transcendence in the attacking play of their teams, but whose impact is not developed in the areas that were once the property of the wingers but as supervening midfielders. Advancing diagonally to the touchline rather than parallel to it, they finish their runs on either side of the midfielder, or in the case of the more positionally aggressive, even in front of the pivot.

This is the case with Ajax's full-backs, whose behaviour in this type of variant is described by Nicolás Tagliafico: "Sometimes we full-backs are almost like a false 10, behind the opposition's midfielders (...) If the opponent plays with two lines of four, with a 1-4-4-2, squares are formed between their defenders and their midfielders. For example, between the full-back, the centre-back, the midfielder and the winger on the right side. So when I appear with that diagonal run inwards, generally nobody can mark me in that square. If a central midfielder comes out, then our striker is going to be able to run to that space in behind; if the full-back comes out, I'm going to create space for our winger; if the winger drops down a lot, it allows my centre-back to move further forward with the ball; and the midfielder can't get too far behind either because then our midfielders will start to receive passes and that's where we start to play them from. It's a move that maybe you're not going to receive the ball, but it's a move that you make to generate concerns for the opposing players".

 Like almost everything else in football, the winger-midfielder is an adjustment with precedents in football in the past, but whose recent revival can be traced back to the period of Pep Guardiola's time at them of Bayern Munich in Germany.

 One of the realities of Guardiola's arrival in the Bundesliga is the realisation that, since his departure from FC Barcelona, his time on the bench would be spent separately from players who were once key to the coach's designs, such as Leo Messi and Xavi Hernández. Over the years, the coach himself admitted that trying to win without them had made him a better coach, as in their absence he had had to take responsibility for aspects, especially in attacking matters, that he had previously been able to delegate to the talent of the two home-grown players. If, as Thierry Henry[121], would later explain, the division of labour during Pep's tenure at the Camp Nou was that the coach took on the task of leading the team into attacking duties, and that the players were left to solve the problem once they were near the opposition's penalty area, away from Barcelona Guardiola acquired more weight, also, in the second part of the plan.

 First and foremost as a result of Thiago Alcântara's recurring injuries in his first season at Bayern, Guardiola realised that the Bavarian squad did not provide him with midfielders with the same level of security when it came to keeping the ball under pressure: "The security in passing that we had in Barcelona we didn't have in Germany. It was very difficult for Barcelona's players to lose the ball

---

121 *Teoría Táctica Fútbol* (12th November, 2018). Henry on Guardiola's game. Extracted from: **https://www.youtube.com/watch?v=ly5La27wx90**

when they were alone or under a bit of pressure. At Bayern I didn't have that specific quality, I had others"[122].

Javi Martínez, Bastian Schweinsteiger or Thomas Müller was a different profile of midfielder, and only Toni Kroos, Heynckes' playmaker who Pep transformed into a playmaker, offered him solutions like those that Xavi, Iniesta and Sergio Busquets at Barça. In this respect, probably one of the most memorable interventions by Guardiola during his time in Germany was the use of Philipp Lahm as a midfielder, a manoeuvre which initially seemed a desperate measure in the face of a shortage of players at the start of 2013-14, but which ultimately established him as a fundamental pillar of the first team that he shaped out of Barcelona. Brazilian Rafinha was his first starting right-back in Germany, because, surprisingly, Lahm turned out to be his trusted midfielder.

"Even Lahm didn't expect it"[123], says Martí Perarnau, author of the book "Herr Pep" and who experienced the German's conversion at the hands of Guardiola. "Philipp lived a second youth. He was happy as a full-back, but when they put him in midfield and he started to play the ball, to move it around... In the first year, talking to him, he told me: this is the moment in my life when I'm enjoying football the most, because now I'm the owner, the ball is constantly going through me. In fact, Lahm was quite angry at the 2014 FIFA World Cup when manager Joachim Löw decided to move him back to full-back. And yet, even so, that World Cup that Germany won I remember Philipp dominating the game from the right. He was like a midfielder on the wing".

According to Martí in his book, during his first season as Bayern head coach, Guardiola did not hesitate to say: "If

---

122 GOL (24th July, 2019). "90 minutes with Pep Guardiola". "*90 minutos con Pep Guardiola*" Extracted from: https://youtu.be/hNCjnwKEea4

123 *En un momento dado* (2021). Interview with Martí Perarnau. Extracted from: https://eumd.es/2021/04/entrevista-marti-perarnau/

we win anything this season, it will be thanks to Lahm. Because it was putting him in central midfield that put all the pieces in order"[124]. And the fact is that, with the German as a rediscovered midfielder, Pep was able to build Toni Kroos, his new conductor, another one of his discoveries in Munich, a more comfortable scenario on the inside left: with a partner for the short combination that, at the same time, would cover his back when he was under pressure. Together with the two of them, Bayern's best stretches of the 2013-14 season were with Thiago as the third vertex of the triangle, although injuries to the Spanish-Brazilian's injuries allowed Bastian Schweinsteiger to play a major role in Guardiola's midfield. "He has taken us to a new tactical level,"[125] Lahm said about the work of head coach Guardiola.

Roman Grill, Philipp's agent, and former Bayern player did not seem to be taken back by surprise by the reinvention of the former full-back. Before becoming his agent, Grill had coached Lahm in the German youth team, playing in midfield: "I think his most important characteristics are his intelligence in the game and his ability to read a game tactically. That's why a player like him has to be in the centre. Philipp brings a lot to defensive organisation, but also to the flow of play. Already as a full-back he had that gift of seeing his team-mate and passing the ball on advantage, which facilitated collective play. But in the midfield position, this ability stands out even more"[126].

Virtues that did not go unnoticed by Guardiola and Domènec Torrent, the coach's assistant and to whom Perarnau attributes the idea of placing Lahm as Bayern's midfielder. "He's one of the most fantastic players I've

---

124 Perarnau, Martí (2014). *Herr Pep. Feature behind the scenes of his first year at Bayern Munich. Crónica desde dentro de su primer año en el Bayern Múnich.* Barcelona, España: Editorial Córner.

125 As (2016). Lahm: "Guardiola has taken us to a new tactical level. "*Guardiola nos ha elevado a un nuevo nivel táctico*". AS newspaper.

ever coaches, and if we're talking about the most intelligent, he's there too. He can calmly play in up to 10 positions, he understands the game perfectly"[127].

"He's beastly intelligent. He picks up everything immediately. He is quick mentally and sees the plays in advance. He has the same level of football intelligence as Iniesta"[128].

A year later, the arrival of Xabi Alonso at Bayern did allow Guardiola to have an organiser in midfield who was in tune with the type or brand of football the team had to play. The presence of the ex-Real Madrid player in the Bavarian pivot area and Lahm's consequent return to right-back, however, did not mean that the team captain and the head coach collapsed the bridge they had built months earlier between the defender and the midfield. In fact, the link was maintained in a twofold sense. Firstly, because after having commanded the German engine room for months, Philipp was able to establish a leadership ability in his play that he continued to develop from the flank, in the manner of a wide organiser; and secondly, because the German has since perfectly embodied one of Guardiola's main tactical innovations in Germany: the aforementioned full-back-midfielders or "*lateriores*"[129].

"You have to have the conditions to fit in, because he likes players to be able to change positions to create uncertainty for the opposition, create space and have control of the game"[130], said Spain international Juan Bernat, one of the full-backs Pep also asked to behave in a differ-

126 Perarnau, Martí (2014). *Herr Pep. Feature behind the scenes of his first year at Bayern Munich. Crónica desde dentro de su primer año en el Bayern Múnich.* Barcelona, España: Editorial Córner.

127 Ballús, Pol (2017). "Guardiola is full of praise for Lahm". "*Guardiola se deshace en elogios a Lahm*". *Sport newspaper.*

128 Perarnau, Martí (2014). *Herr Pep. Feature behind the scenes of his first year at Bayern Munich. Crónica desde dentro de su primer año en el Bayern Múnich.* Barcelona, España: Editorial Córner.

129 Morén, Albert (2016). *En un momento dado*: The 'lateriores' of Guardiola. *Los lateriores de Guardiola.* Extracted from: https://eumd.es/2016/09/analisis-papel-laterales-manchester-city-guardiola/

ent way than usual. These were players lined up as full-backs, who when the team defended close to their area had to act like full-backs, containing opposition attacks on either side of the back four. But both with the ball in Bayern's possession and when the German team lost the ball close to the opposition goal, they were to look like as inside midfielders. They were transformed into midfielders. In attack, therefore, they did not project out wide to capitalise on the outside threat or share it with the winger, but inwards. Their route was not in a straight line but in a diagonal that ended up placing them on the flanks of the midfielder. They started to play as Cafú, Maicon, Roberto Carlos or Maldini, but they finished it like Xavi, Luka Modrić, Kroos, Clarence Seedorf, Cesc Fàbregas or Edgar Davids.

In addition to the pivot zone, Lahm, Alaba, Rafinha or Juan Bernat were to provide extra protection for their occupant, without their presence in the team's engine room making them less agile. Without the ball they would retain their defensive qualities, but with it they had to pass as consummate midfielders. Interpret the game, play quickly and accurately, orient themselves correctly, spread out on the pitch to generate passing options and flow in the interchange of positions. At the same time, bringing them close to the ball in attack meant that when the team lost possession their situation was equally close to the ball, thus distinguishing themselves as two vital elements in defensive management when switching from attacking to defending. Guarding the backs of two attacking inside backs, reinforcing both sides of the midfield and with the reading provided by their experience as defenders ready to give them an advantage in the pressure, when it came to disputing clearances or cutting off the opposition's counterattacks.

"Guardiola was often looking for that: for the full-back to have a more inside game in attack and that for any loss of the ball he could be close enough to press, steal and start playing again", Zabaleta, who worked under the Catalan coach during the 2016-2017 season, added: "Pep always looked for depth with the wingers and for the full-back to come inside when the ball was lost to generate interior superiority. (...), I would have liked to have 26 or 27 years old and in my prime when Guardiola came to Manchester City, so I could have enjoyed a bit more with him. He's a very innovative and very detailed coach. He really likes attacking play and he always prepares the team to attack".

Pep did not enjoy Leo Messi in Germany either. Instead Bayern Munich had a different type of striker, more canonical and easier to fit into the classic scheme of wingers and centre-forwards. Having Robben, Ribéry, Coman, Douglas Costa, Mandzukić or Lewandowski where he had the Argentinian, forced Guardiola to work his team's attack in a different way, and to try to promote different game situations. Looking for one-on-ones on the wings and conquering the flanks to deliver the cross into the box required a different kind of collective conditioning.

On the one hand, it was essential to find the wing forwards as high up the pitch as possible and in a position to face their opponents one-on-one. Open on the flanks and without the appearance of the full-back bringing a second defender closer to their area. In this sense, when it came to clearing the ball, the use of the full-backs was going to be of great help. Firstly because with their runs they would drag the opposing wingers inside, and secondly because by crossing to the opposing wingers they would also help the Bayern centre-backs to find the wide forward with a long pass. There would be no obstacle between the centre-back and the German winger. The goal would be closer: to get the ball as early and as high as possible to the feet of the team's most dangerous and decisive players as early and as high as possible.

"The key is that the end and the side of the same side are never in the same flank (...). The idea is to have the centre-back open, the full-back on the inside and the winger open to pass directly to him. If the pass goes well you have the whole of the enemy's midfield; if you lose the ball, your full-back can close down the space immediately (...). Our full-back goes to the centre and drags the opposing winger; if he doesn't follow him, then you have a free man"[131].

Secondly, the role and importance of Bayern's wingers in attack invited a new behaviour (or at least more marked from then on) of the inside players in Guardiola's script. Coming from the second line to join up with the nine in the box waiting for the lateral cross or attacking with and without the ball the space between the opposing full-backs held close to the whitewash. A pair of inside players that often took on the appearance of an attacking midfielder, or one that even looked like resuscitating the old pyramid-shaped-five-pronged attacking formation of five forwards: "Look at me, the standard-bearer of midfielders, playing with five forwards! All my life I've been arguing that you have to play with midfielders, that the key is in the midfield, and now I've got the strength in the forwards... But be careful! It's not just putting strikers in for the sake of it (...), the key is in the two full-backs, who when they have the ball in front of them, they close down next to the midfield and form a line of three that protects us against counter-attacks. With this lifeline it's possible to put five forwards because you have your backs covered"[132].

In order for everything to be sustainable, and for the offensive projection of the interiors did not result in a dangerous emptying of the midfield, again the centralised participation of both full-backs provided the perfect tactical support: "If we have the ball, we're vertical from the position created by Alaba and Rafinha. If we lose the ball,

---

130 Palomo, David (2015). Juan Bernat: "I wish it was only about stopping Messi". *'Ojalá solo se tratase de parar a Messi'*. *El Mundo* newspaper.

131 Perarnau, Martí (2014). *Herr Pep. Feature behind the scenes of his first year at Bayern Munich. Crónica desde dentro de su primer año en el Bayern Múnich.* Barcelona, España: Editorial Córner.

we have all the players positioned in the centre and very high up: it will be easy to win the ball back"[133].

Tite, the Brazilian national team head coach, must have been thinking along similar lines during the 2019 Copa America, when in attack he used Dani Alves and Filipe Luis played the ball on the inside despite their initial position as full-backs"[134]. Or coaches Jorge Almirón or Marcelo Gallardo, who in Argentinian football put the same type of operation into practice employing José Luis Gómez and Maxi Velázquez in the case for the former Lanús head coach, or by employing Camilo Mayada and Milton Casco in the case for the head coach of River Plate[135].

The last variation Pep though of during his time at Barcelona[136], was to bring the full-backs inside and not on the wing, although his departure from the Camp Nou forced him to postpone its implementation until his arrival in Munich. Two decades earlier, still as an active footballer, the Santpedor-born coach had been able to see first-hand the functioning and the effects of this particular behaviours of the full-backs, as a member of the Dream Team led by Johan Cruyff that made Barça history. "When I'm in doubt," Guardiola confesses, "I always think: what would Johan do?"[137].

132 Perarnau, Martí (2016). *Pep Guardiola. The metamorphosis. "Pep Guardiola. La metamorfosis"*. Barcelona, España: Editorial Córner.

133 Perarnau, Martí (2014), *Herr Pep. Feature behind the scenes of his first year at Bayern Munich. Crónica desde dentro de su primer año en el Bayern Múnich*. Barcelona, España: Editorial Córner.

134 Parra Peña, Javier [@Javier_EPP] (2 de julio, 2019). Analizo los roles y funciones de Dani Alves y Filipe Luis dentro del sistema de juego de la Brasil de Tité [Tuit]. Twitter. https://twitter.com/Javier_EPP/status/1146078298075779073.

135 Muglia, Vicente (2019). The "lateriores" have arrived. *Llegaron los lateriores. Olé* newspaper.

136 Perarnau, Martí (2014). *Herr Pep. Feature behind the scenes of his first year at Bayern Munich. Crónica desde dentro de su primer año en el Bayern Múnich*. Barcelona, España: Editorial Córner.

137 Juanmartí, Toni (2017). Guardiola: "When I'm in doubt, I always think: what would Johan do"? *"Cuando dudo, siempre pienso: '¿Qué haría Johan?'". Sport* newspaper.

In this case, the use of the "*lateriores*" was not a recurrent resource used in the tactical approaches by the Dutch manager, but it was an alternative used in specific matches. For example, using Albert Ferrer in this way so that his abilities as a marker could be better directed at an inside threat from the opposition, such as Atlético Madrid's Milinko Pantić in 1995 or the Juventus pairing of Roberto Baggio and Thomas Hässler in 1991. On the 26th of February 1994, not only Ferrer but also Sergi Barjuán, on the left flank, played the role of inside full-back in Cruyff or "*el Flaco*'s" team. On that day, Cruyff's Barça took on Deportivo La Coruña, a side that under manager Arsenio Iglesias had earned the nickname "*Super Dépor*" and that night appeared at the Camp Nou as league leaders. The Catalans would eventually win 3 goals to 0 to move closer to the top of La Liga, thanks to goals from Stoichkov, Romário and Laudrup, and an approach in which Johan's role for his full-backs was outstanding. With the ball for Barça, their mission was to join in the attack through the centre, dragging the vigilance of the Galicians' wide strikers, thus allowing Ronald Koeman and Miguel Ángel Nadal to Eusebio and Iván Iglesias on the wing.

In fact, Eusebio Sacristán himself was used by Cruyff in the full-back position for some stretches of the *Dream Team* cycle, with the aim of using his midfield virtues to start the game. "We used a 1-3-4-3 with a midfield diamond. The pivot was Guardiola, the central midfielder was Koeman, and we had two full-backs like Ferrer, Sergi or Juan Carlos who were very quick but perhaps their best virtue wasn't playing the ball out of the box. There was a moment when the opponents were playing us in 1-4-4-1-1 with the aim of putting a fixed mark on the midfielder, who was Guardiola, and another on the centre-back with the best outlet, who was Koeman. And when the opponents started to do that, Johan came up with the idea of putting me at full-back instead of inside, because it allowed me to come out with the ball and start the game. I

could give those inside passes to Laudrup, or to the winger for Goikoetxea, or connect with the striker. That was the idea"[138].

Luis Cembranos, who was a youth player at the time, also played the same role when Cruyff called him up for the first team: "The objective was to have a better outlet for the ball. Unlike a midfielder, when I played as a full-back I could have more vision of the field and play with the ball at the start of the action"[139], recalls the Spanish international. During the 1994-1995 season, Cembranos played at right-back for Barça in a Champions League match at Old Trafford, on a night in which, precisely, he was replaced in the second half by Eusebio Sacristán.

Like Eusebio and Luis Cembranos in their time, many other modern-day laterals or full-backs have made the same journey from midfield to defence, pushed by the weight in the management of the game that the more backward positions have also in the more defensive positions. It is easier to find the attributes in terms of vision of play, clean outlet and movement management that certain principles of modern football demand of them, in those who have been occupying the positions where these functions used to fall exclusively to them.

This is what happened in Barcelona in the case of Sergi Roberto, midfielders trained at La Masía, whose conversion to a full-back Luis Enrique referred in these terms, "You have to have a great physique, you have to have technical concepts and footballing quality on a technical level to know what kind of game you have to play... normally a player who delays his position starts to see the situations and that's a big advantage for Sergi". Or that of Fabian Delph and Oleksandr Zinchenko, a habitual or

138 *En un momento dado* (2021). Interview with Eusebio Sacristán. Extracted from: https://eumd.es/2021/04/entrevista-eusebio-sacristan/

139 Morén, Albert (2019). *En un momento dado*: About full-backs and attacking midfielders. *Sobre laterales e interiores*. Extracted from: https://eumd.es/2019/08/analisis-relacion-laterales-interiores/

playmaker that despite the occasional dabble at full-back when he played for Russia[140], who Pep Guardiola normally used as a full-back at City. "He is talented and a very intelligent player. Because of the way he plays, his decisions are always perfect"[141].

Sergi Roberto, Delph and Zinchenko are three examples of footballers, who, despite having played as midfielders for most of their careers, have found a place at the top level as a full-back. For other names, the move to the defensive position has not taken on the same permanent character but appears as an occasional resource that their coaches use in very specific playing contexts. This was the case for Ander Herrera during the 2019-2020 when Tuchel called on him in some games to play at right-back for Paris Saint-Germain.

"I like to give the coaches options and be useful. The times I've played as a full-back, in many moments of the game I was practically a midfielder. And as usual, because of the quality we have in the team, we control the game and have possession, it's easier for a midfielder to become a full-back for a day (...). I think it's a very good solution, and Guardiola has pioneered it (...). The fact of putting the full-backs practically as midfielders at a given moment of the game, makes the winger and the opposing team's inside players very doubtful. They don't know whether to go or not, because normally the wingers go to press the full-backs, but if they are going inside, they don't have a full-back to press. I find it a fantastic solution.

Full-backs are having more and more influence on the game. It's one of the things I've seen in the evolution of

---

140 Bajkowski, Simon (2017). The Pep Guardiola talk that transformed Zinchenko's Man City career. *Manchester Evening News*. Extracted from: https://www.manchestereveningnews.co.uk/sport/football/football-news/man-city-zinchenko-left-back-16842639

141 Sadhanand, Srinivas (2018). *El Arte del Fútbol*: From Benchwarmer To Title Winner. The Rise Of Zinchenko. Extracted from: www.elartedf.com/the-rise-of-oleksandr-zinchenko/

football over the last ten years (...). Especially in the last years of his career, Dani Alves has been more of a midfielder. A player who gives continuity to the game from the wing, and perhaps the most influential player in football from this position in the last ten or fifteen years. He can be a good example for any midfielder who at any given moment is going to play at full-back (...), I think he is the clearest example that from full-back you can be very influential in the game"[142].

Another essential name in the transition from midfield to full-back is David Alaba, who Jupp Heynckes first converted into a deep, wide left-back, and then under Guardiola, like Philipp Lahm, changed his game to a more inside midfield influence. "I've gradually adapted. Now I'm more involved in attacking play. These are small details, but they have a big impact on the way I approach games. I'm trying to do what my team is doing. My aim is to do what the coach expects of me and to be happy"[143]. As a full-back, centre-back or midfielder, Alaba often played in a mixture of all three positions under the Catalan coach. "He can play in absolutely any position"[144], Guardiola said of him, happy to take advantage of his imposing physical ability, his technical skills, and his tactical intelligence to intervene in the game in a variety of ways and in the most varied areas. A multi-functional full-back, capable of playing on the wing and in the centre, of taking part in the first passes or waiting for play from more advanced positions. "I have yet to understand in which position Alaba played tonight"[145], Italy's late 1982 World Cup winner had to confess after a Bayern Munich display against AS Roma that ended in a 7-1 thumping win.

---

142 *En un momento dado* (2021). Interview with Ander Herrera. Extracted from: https://eumd.es/2021/04/entrevista-ander-herrera/

143 Palomo, David (2013). "Alaba is a gift". "*Alaba es un regalo*". *El Mundo.*

144 As (2016). David Alaba: "Pep Guardiola has reinvented football". "*Pep Guardiola ha reinventado el fútbol*". *As newspaper.*

145 Honigstein, Raphael (2016). David Alaba: "I didn't know I could play as a central defender". *The Guardian.*

The fact that the full-back breaks into a space where he is not expected in order to create uncertainty for the opposing defensive system is one of the keys to the variant. It is also a reason for those in charge to adapt, as it places them in different playing contexts to those, they have traditionally been familiar with. "You have to train and practise a lot because that area is not what we full-backs are used to", explains Tagliafico. (...) "You have to work on angles and the side you are facing, control of the ball and peripheral vision. We're used to playing facing the ball, and playing on the inside, opponents can come at you from either side. Before receiving you have to look where you can escape to or where they can come at you from".

Zabaleta is along the same lines when he comments that "on the inside, when you receive the pass from the centre-back and you are not well profiled, if you lose the ball the whole team is open, and it can be a problem. It's different if you lose it on the wing. It's less dangerous there. That's why we used to train that a lot with Pep. And if the full-backs went inside but we were under pressure, the centre-back tried to play with the striker, with the winger or look for other options".

"I feel more comfortable going out wide," confesses Pablo Maffeo. "On the inside it's more difficult for me because it's a space where I'm not used to receiving balls on and on the outside, as I'm a physically powerful player and it's an area I've been used to for many years, I feel more confident and if things get difficult, I know what I have to do". The full-back, who came through the youth ranks at Manchester City in the summer of 2013, adds that "Guardiola taught me a lot in the short time I was with him. I learnt concepts that I still apply today and that make me improve (...). He insisted a lot on my body position when I was going to receive the ball. Or to control with one leg and pass with the other to gain time. Small details that can make a difference in the end".

It is probably because of this difficulty in receiving the ball in an orientated position that a player who is used to moving in these areas of the pitch as a midfielder will find it easier to apply himself as a full-back, as happened to Ander Herrera in his experience as a right-back at PSG: "When the left centre-back has the ball and you get into the line of midfielders as a full-back, it is true that, although perhaps not completely backwards, you can find yourself a little diagonally when receiving the ball. And logically a midfielder is more used to doing that".

At Bayern Munich, too, after Guardiola's departure and the retirement of Philipp Lahm, another midfielder, Joshua Kimmich, took over at right-back[146]. "Pep showed me completely new spaces on the pitch. I improved a lot. He cares a lot about your first touch and that you know what to do even before you receive the ball. You have to know where your team-mates are, so he wants you to scan the whole pitch"[147]. In his case, however, because his first few seasons at Bayern still coincided with Lahm's presence in the squad, the conversion he initially starred in saw him play as a surprise centre-back, before finding his new home at right-back orphaned by the iconic captain. "My favourite position is midfield (...), in Germany, since the European Championships, I play mainly as a right-back, but sometimes also as a centre-back in a back three (...), but whatever position I play in, I try to play in my own style. I don't just defend. I want to create chances and, if I can, I also want to score. You have to find the right balance, and for a young player it's important not to try to copy anyone and be yourself".

""He has everything to be the second Lahm (...). He understands the tactics, the phases of the game and knows when to change the tempo," predicted Paul Breitner, a his-

---

146 Pineda, Rafael (2016). Kimmich, the guinea pig football player. *El País newspaper*.

147 McRae, Donald (2018). Joshua Kimmich: "I want to be me, not a Lahm clone or Lahm the second". *The Guardian*.

toric former Bayern and German national team player who, a few decades before Kimmich or Alaba, also walked the path between midfield and full-back. "I was the pioneer," said the former Germany star of the 1974 World Cup-winning side in an interview with El País newspaper[148].

"In Hannover, at the beginning of 1971. I was a midfielder at Bayern and five hours before the game Udo Lattek asked me: 'Paul, we have a lot of injured players, do me a favour and play as a full-back. I never wanted to be a full-back. It disgusted me. Full-backs were tough guys who only had to mark an opponent with no other rights than to defend. I interpreted the position in my own way. Udo Lattek said he'd never seen anyone play so well in that position. In that Hannover-Bayern game, Lahm, Kimmich, Jordi Alba, Alaba, Ramos were born... In every country we see players like that: when they are tidy, they are full-backs and when the chaos starts they are midfielders or forwards. It was a change in terms of rights: that day the full-backs acquired more rights. You can't play good football without full-backs like Lahm".

---

148 Torres, Diego (2018). "Germany understood that the only successful football was that played by Barça and Spain". "*Alemania entendió que el único fútbol de éxito era el que jugaban el Barça y España*". *El País newspaper.*

CHAPTER 5

CENTRAL DEFENDERS IN THE OUTDOORS

> "Guardiola has ruined Italian defenders. There aren't any more centre-backs like Maldini, Baresi or Cannavaro"[149]
>
> GIORGIO CHIELLINI

Until 2020, Pep Guardiola had won 9 out of 12 Liga titles that his team had contested. One at Barça B, the prelude to gaining promotion to the third division of Spanish football, three with the first team at FC Barcelona, another three with Bayern Munich and, up until now at the time of writing this book, two with Manchester City. His teams reached five of those 9 titles as the highest-scoring team in the competition, a feat consistent with the distinctly attacking character and nature proposed by the coach and with the sheer talent of his attacking football players.

---

149 *El Periódico* (2017). Chiellini: "Guardiola has ruined Italian defenders". "*Guardiola ha arruinado a los defensas italianos*". *El Periódico newspaper.*

That's why, because the overall picture of Pep Guardiola's football has more to do with what his players do when they have the ball and what happens during matches in the vicinity of the opponent's penalty area, it is probably more surprising that of the nine league titles to his teams' credit, as many as seven were won by being the lowest goals conceded teams in the league. Only UE Sant Andreu in the coach's debut season, (competing in Group 5 of Spain's semi-professional third division) and Liverpool under Jürgen Klopp, who ended the 2018-2019 season one point behind Manchester City, and having conceded only one goal less than the champions, have disputed the direct relationship between Guardiola's leagues and the safety of his teams.

From this perspective, Guardiola's curriculum would make for a good motto, widely repeated in football as in other sports that, attacks win games, but defences win titles. Guardiola himself has stated on occasion that the phase of the game that receives the most attention in his training sessions is precisely the defence.

It happens that in several aspects in Guardiola's footballing ideology, the defence responds to different coordinates from those in which it is traditionally pigeonholed. Preferably, it does not happen near the own area but far from the goalkeeper, it speaks through a fierce pressure that relies on the advanced position of all the members of the team and drinks directly from the contexts of play generated previously with the ball.

His teams want to contain the ball up top, running towards the opponent's goal and not back towards their own, bringing as many players as possible close to the ball so that the reaction after losing the ball is more immediate and effective, and after the circulation of the ball has generated disorder in their opponents. Their aim is to make it difficult for the opposing players to find each other on the pitch in order to move forward in sync. Defending almost as a way of attacking and attacking almost as a way of defending.

Since his is a different way of defending, the players, and the functions they perform must also be different, which is why, under his tutelage and influence, the players who have been part of his systems have had to adapt. Especially those who initially focused their game on the defensive line. Goalkeepers, full-backs, and centre-backs have been forced to change. Firstly because their offensive responsibility has increased and, secondly, because the defensive functions that their position incorporates have been transferred to other areas of the pitch and under different playing parameters. This is confirmed by Juan Carlos Unzué, when he states that "the positions that have changed the most since I started as a player are goalkeeper and centre-back. For me, they are the two positions that have changed the most, because the number and variety of situations they have to dominate has increased"[150].

These are positions that have undergone a revolution that has left behind principles that once seemed immovable, both in terms of the individual characteristics of their protagonists and their relationships with their teammates. In this respect, for example, the idea of shaping the centre-back pairing from the sum of different and therefore complementary profiles was an idea that was particularly ingrained in the footballing imagination for years. In a position that is so closely linked to a partner or team-mate, where it is generally the combination of the two centre-backs is generally expected to be more than the sum of their individual players, the cabal about the best possible fit for them often takes on a very high relevance when the last protective barrier is built in front of the goalkeeper.

Thus, traditionally, the prevailing tendency has been to try to form combinations of exclusive virtues, in order to

---

150 *En un momento dado* (2021). Interview with Juan Carlos Unzué. Extracted from: https://eumd.es/2021/04/entrevista-juan-carlos-unzue/

cover with two players the full spectrum of characteristics that a centre-back can have. The virtues that define one of the members of the pair are those that are lacking in the other, and vice versa. Next to a more positional and less quick defender, a quicker and more battle-hardened one, especially suited to correction, would be placed. Next to an orderly defender, with reading and personality to position his team-mates, an expert in individual battles and vigilance over the striker. Alongside a solid marker without many virtues when it came to playing the ball, a partner of superior technical ability and fine-tuned vision.

"I was a centre-back who tried to come out with the ball. I wasn't very physical for a marking centre-back and they usually put me next to a more physical centre-back who was stronger in marking", recalls Gerard Autet, who trained as a centre-back in the youth ranks at FC Barcelona and who, after leaving La Masía, alternated between 2001 and 2011 in the Spanish first and second divisions with Espanyol, Levante, Xerez and Sporting de Gijón[151].

Rafa Márquez and Gerard Piqué, one of the first pairings used by Guardiola after his arrival to the Barça first team bench, proposed a different canon. On the 4th of October 2008, the Catalan coach's young project welcomed Atlético Madrid to the Camp Nou. After the unexpected early stumbles against Numancia and Racing Santander, the Culé side had managed to string together three consecutive wins in La Liga and two in the Champions League, but the visit of the team coached by Javier Aguirre looked to be the most demanding match to date for the Blaugrana. Despite the absence of Diego Forlán, the "*rojiblanco*" attack would be the first great threat of the season for a Barça side that had still not managed to keep a clean sheet, with Sergio "Kun" Agüero leading the way accompanied by Florent Sinama-Pongolle on a scoring

---

151 *En un momento dado* (2021). Interview with Gerard Autet. Extracted from: https://eumd.es/2021/04/entrevista-gerard-autet/

streak. Two fast strikers who their team could use on the counter-attack and with the ability to punish the daring of an opponent who placed the defence far from their own goal. Two strikers with whom to force the opposing centre-backs to run backwards, imposing their superior pace in open spaces.

However, to stop them Pep Guardiola did not use any of the sprinters on offer in the squad. Abidal and Puyol started the game defending the full-backs and Martín Cáceres from the bench, leaving Piqué and Márquez in the centre of defence. Together they would form a pair of similar profiles, being both two centre-backs more positional, lucid in initiating play and less prepared to correct from the physical exuberance of their physical defensive situations. Asked beforehand about the recipe or solution for containing Atlético Madrid's dangerous strikers, Guardiola had already hinted at his intentions: "to know where they move, try to dominate the game so that they intervene as little as possible and avoid their counter-attacks".

Barça's defensive mission would not be to stop opposing attackers, but to disable them. Intervening before they appeared and, when they did, to ensure that their participation would be in the most unfavourable conditions possible. Rafa Márquez ad Gerard Piqué were not to impose themselves directly on the forwards, but rather to intervene before they appeared directly on the strikers, but to contribute their good work with the ball and their right positioning on the pitch the field, to ensure that the "*Colchoneros*" enjoyed the ball for as little time as possible, and that when they did have the ball it was far away from Valdés' area. Leaving Agüero and Sinama-Pongolle without passes or balls fed to them and obliged to intervene in areas of the pitch from which they could not generate danger. "If you don't lose the ball in the build-up phase, it's very difficult to be counter-attacked," said Johan Cruyff, and no matter how decisive Atlético Madrid's

forwards were, they couldn't score playing in midfield and without touching the ball.

A formula, to which Guardiola would also give continuity with more orthodox defensive profiles such as Carles Puyol, Jérôme Boateng, Nicolás Otamendi or Rúben Dias, which entailed a change of priorities in defensive matters and, consequently a new paradigm for the centre-back position. Defenders carved by the pattern of different demands in attack but also in defence, far removed from the sketchy portrait that for years the players in the position had responded to.

One of the latest examples, Giorgio Chiellini, and his historic fellow countrymen like Claudio Gentile, Gaetano Scirea, Franco Baresi, Giuseppe Bergomi, Paolo Maldini, Alessandro Nesta and Fabio Cannavaro, interviewed by *Gazzetta dello Sport* in 2018, lamented that "now everyone looks up, in crosses there are no more defenders who intimidate the opposition (...). Now all the defenders know how to organise themselves, but they don't know how to mark the striker. When I was young, I used to train myself to 'feel the man', marking well in the penalty area... That doesn't exist now. Today's Italian defenders leave everyone free. It's a pity that the essence of a school is being lost"[152].

Mauricio Pochettino explained something similar to Guillem Balagué about the new generations of footballers. The Argentinian, now coach after a long career as a central defender in Argentina, Spain and France, illustrated the difference between eras in what for so many years was his position: "One of the things that worries us and that we discussed at Tottenham is that sometimes players lack those basic concepts (...). A central defender who doesn't make fouls! Before, if you didn't foul, you couldn't play as

---

152 *La Gazzetta dello Sport* (2018). Chiellini: "Top season. The World Cup? I don't watch it. And Guardiola has ruined us". "*Stagione al top. Mondiale? Non guardo. E Guardiola ci ha rovinati*". *La Gazzetta dello Sport* newspaper.

a centre-back. Twenty years ago, if you didn't play hard and mark the line, the forwards would eat you up (...). Now the defender who doesn't foul is the best. Fuck me! How different is it today, it has changed, hasn't it?"[153].

His compatriot and former Argentina international team-mate Diego Pablo Simeone, asked about his work at Atlético Madrid, also responded that "every day there are better players in football, but they are worse at defending. Teams defend worse, and those that defend better are the ones that end up winning. They all have good players up front; they all have good attacking players because in the best teams in the world you are going to have good attacking players. The problem, now, is knowing how to defend. Because if you know how to defend, you're always going to have a chance of scoring a goal. But how many teams know how to defend?"[154].

"Where I think there is a big difference between the defender of the past and the defenders of today is that we used to enjoy defending," adds Paco Jémez on this issue. The Spaniard, one of La Liga's iconic centre-backs of the 1990s, fought his way through the Primera División as part of the defences of Rayo Vallecano, Deportivo de La Coruña, Real Zaragoza and the national team, before embarking on a coaching career marked by a very attacking approach to the game, more linked to the opposition's penalty area than his own. Despite the daring and pro-active style with the ball that he now tries to instil in his teams, when Jémez looks back at his playing days, he is reminded of a trait that he no longer finds: the pleasure of defending.

"I used to enjoy beating the striker, proving that I was better than him. Nowadays I don't see that so much. I think

153 Balagué, G. and Pochettino, M. (2018). A new world. An intimate diary of Pochettino in London.. *Un mundo nuevo. Diario íntimo de Pochettino en Londres.* Barcelona, España: Editorial Contra.

154 FOX Sports Sur (2019). *90 Minutos.* Interview with Diego *"Cholo"* Simeone.

the mentality of the defender has changed completely, and that's why I think they are worse defenders now than they used to be. They have better conditions, because they are faster, they are stronger, they are more agile, but I think that the love that we used to have for defending has been lost a lot.

When I faced Ismael Urzaiz, I enjoyed it a lot. I was the happiest man in the world. He was a striker who was six foot tall, weighed almost a hundred kilos and was an animal, but I loved playing against him because he was noble. We knew what we were going for and, although we were team-mates in the national team, on the pitch we used to beat the shit out of each other. They were fights with pride and honour. I remember them with great affection.

There were other ways of defending and, above all, different demands from the coaches. What the coach asked of me was that the opposing striker didn't score goals. That was all. I knew that they were going to count on me depending on whether I scored well against the opposing striker. That has changed and the players have also had to adapt to the new demands of modern football"[155].

Gerard Autet also refers to these different demands to which Jémez refers when he compares the type of defensive situations to which he is exposed. I don't think that defending is worse than before, but rather that the centre-back is asked to do so many things that sometimes he loses a certain practically. Defenders now have a lot of responsibilities. They have to come out with the ball in play, they have to be quick, intelligent, communicate with their team-mates to coordinate the line, go out to cover the full-back run many metres back, ve very physically prepared...".

One of the most conditioning aspects when it comes to generating a different type of scenario for centre-backs,

---

155 *En un momento dado* (2021). Interview with Paco Jémez. Extracted from: https://eumd.es/2021/04/entrevista-paco-jemez/

is the tendency of teams to position the defensive line far away from the box. Assuming the risk of conceding metres at the back and relying on the help of the goalkeepers outside the box, managing the space between the backline and the goal, the desire to press in the opposition's half and to keep the team together around the ball has meant that, in many moments has meant that, at many times, the role of centre-back is no longer a job confined to the penalty area. Not only with the ball, they need to offer guarantees at midfield level, but also that their role in containment has shifted away from the goal. The centre-back must defend in midfield, with no other lifeline than the cover of his goalkeeper and exposing himself to direct attacks from the opponent attacking directly behind him. Instead of reducing space at the back, he reduces it forwards.

On this issue, from his experience first as a central defender and later as a coach adept attacking football, Paco Jémez assumed that "any defender who has a lot of space behind him or to his sides takes a risk. The strikers are quick and if they get away from their markers, they practically stay in front of the goalkeeper. That's the risk you take playing like that because you have many other advantages".

Autet agrees with the positive balance that the combination of risk-taking by centre-backs and between the risk taken and the benefits that this type of play has for the team: "The best way to protect yourself is to compress the team forward. That's why you need brave and quicker centre-backs so they can react when the team loses the ball".

Consequently, issues such as the coordination to draw the offside line, the agility to turn on one's axis when the play requires one to drop back, and the ability to run into the open field in a direct duel at speed against the striker, have been added to their repertoire. There is also a demand for physiques that are better equipped to survive exposure, and for personalities that are comfortable with the reality of a more risk-taking role. What was once shelter inside the box and surrounded by team-mates is now unprotected in very advanced defences. The space that decades ago served as a refuge for veteran defenders or midfielders who, as they got older, moved back in the pitch to play in a more protected position, is now an open space on a technical, tactical, physical and mental level.

Within the new defensive ecosystem that welcomes central defenders, one of the actions that has multiplied its value is defensive surveillance, i.e. the monitoring that the central defender does on an opposing attacker while his team-mates are moving away from the attack, in order to be able to give the best possible response in the event that the ball changes sides and the opponent is intent on quickly punishing the spaces with his more advanced players.

Therefore, in a football that increasingly asks centre-backs to develop their play away form their own area, Autet considers that "defensive vigilance is becoming more and more important (...). Before, we used to look for a free defender just in case, but nowadays we often mark man-to-man. The rigour of defensive surveillance is fundamental. As a centre-back you can't just watch the game when you don't have the ball, you have to keep living the game. Look for your mark and adjust your position on the pitch".

It's the same idea that Jémez is pointing out when he insists that, even when the game takes place far away from his area, the attitude of the centre-back cannot be contemplative: "They have to be very attentive to defensive vigilance. That's where defenders sometimes make mistakes because they are watching the game. When the team has the ball in the end zone, the centre-backs cannot be mere spectators, their job is to be well positioned and close to the last striker in case there is a counter-attack or a long ball. Centre-backs are never spectators".

However, the increased space that centre-backs have to take care of is not only related to the height of the defensive line and the metres behind them that separate them from the goalkeeper. In defensive recipes more related to the retreat and the conjuring in one's own area, for example, the proximity and functions of the midfielder served as a barricade. As a first parapet located a few metres in front, who could even, at many moments of the play, delay is to position himself as a third centre-back to reinforce his area. Defensive pressing systems, on the other hand, base their response when they don't have the ball on players moving forward, to get closer to the ball and the opponents in a position to play it. Following this commandment, therefore, it is also common for the pivots to defend by running in the direction of the opposing goal, separating themselves from the back line and increasing the distance from the position of the centre-backs.

Thirdly, the weight and attacking presence that the full-backs have acquired, either by joining the attack on the wing or breaking into the central lane, often also strips the wings of the defence, enlarging the area for which the centre-backs are responsible towards the flanks. "It used to be said that if one full-back went forward, the other had to stay back. And that guaranteed that there would always be at least three defenders at the back. Now, in many moments, the full-backs are on top", Autet adds. Where teams used to employ full-backs whose involvement in attack was, as a rule, secondary, and who used to alternate with their opposite number so that one of the two always stayed at the back, today football is discovering players with an enormous offensive impact and whose appearance in attacking areas often occurs at the same time as that of the other full-back.

In a game in which it is no longer anecdotal for a right-back to score from the left-back's cross from the by-line, the defensive link between centre-backs and the wing has become closer. Unlike what happens with the inside spaces, they also do so without the goalkeeper being able to intervene as naturally as when he provides cover behind the centre-backs, as Jémez explains: "For me, the space behind the centre-backs doesn't worry me so much because I always have the goalkeeper there, who can act as a sweeper for any long ball. But it's true that on the sides of the centre-backs there is still a lot of space, and any ball that goes there can be a problem, because on lateral balls the goalkeeper has less influence. A forward ball will normally go close to the goalkeeper, but a long ball to the flanks creates more uncertainty".

For this reason, both Paco Jémez and Gerard Autet agree that it is more difficult for a centre-back to cover on the wing, having to go out to the theoretical area of the full-back, abandoning his starting position. "It generates more insecurity," admits Autet, "because on the inside you feel you dominate your area, you know the area, you respond to a lateral cross. But if you have to go out to the wing and the opposition winger faces you, you feel more vulnerable. It's a more uncomfortable situation".

Due to the amount of space that centre-backs have to cover when their team loses the ball, and the demands that this scenario makes on their speed, power and agility, it was possible that the evolution of the position could be oriented towards the consolidation of a physical profile similar to that of the full-backs. Players who are fast, light, skilful, elastic, with a high capacity for reaction, change of pace, adapted to playing in large spaces and responding by appearing on the wing. However, and although the decade points to examples such as Carles Puyol, Eric Abidal, David Alaba, Javier Mascherano, Samuel Umtiti, Lisandro Martínez and Jules Koundé, the position is still dominated by full-bodied defenders. Centre-backs who are physically prepared for their new playing contexts, but who not only maintain the stature of their predecessors, but even increase it.

For years, this has been the case with Képler Laveran, better known in the football world as Pepe. The centre-back arrived in 2007 at a Real Madrid where team-mates such as Christoph Metzelder and World Cup winner Fabio Cannavaro gave voice to the type of centre-back that was the norm, a model of defender reinforced inside his own area, in charge of guarding small areas and sheltered by the accumulation of players around him. Pepe, however, was the opposite, for as Abel Rojas described him in his article "Pepe: A before and an after", thanks to his speed the Brazilian was "a marker who grew as he moved away from his goal and himself meant an advantage, because if he missed, the time the striker had to spend to get to the goal was the seconds he used to return to the play"[156].

Juande Ramos, who coached him for a few months as Real Madrid manager points out that for that Real Madrid *"he was an essential player. For big teams that play a long way out of the box, having fast defenders is fundamental, and Pepe was that. He was the quickest in defence"*[157]. It was a speed that later helped José Mourinho to design his response to the Barça team of Leo Messi and Pep Guardiola: a backline with a tendency to cut back, that is, to reduce the space for the opposition by going forward, led by centre-back pairing of Pepe and Sergio Ramos. A tandem capable of moving forward to defend the back of the midfield, position to defend the back of the midfield, and at the same time, correct by speed the threats at their back.

The popularity of defensive systems based on pressing in the opposition half and the forward positioning of all lines of the team, as a method of confronting positional attacking approaches and elaborate ball control, has extended the trend. Jürgen Klopp's Liverpool is one of its

---

156 Rojas, Abel (2017). *Ecos del balón*: Pepe. A before and an after. Extracted from: http://www.ecosdelbalon.com/2017/06/analisis-tactico-pepe-influencia-historia-real-madrid/

157 *En un momento dado* (2021). Interview with Juande Ramos. Extracted from: https://eumd.es/2021/04/entrevista-juande-ramos/

most iconic exponents, as the flagship of a "gegenpressing" that earned the Reds the Champions League in 2019 and the Premier League in 2020, and at the heart of which is a 193-centimetre-tall centre-back. However, for Virgil van Dijk, winner of the 2019 UEFA Men's Player of the Year Award that honoured him as the best player in Europe as judged by UEFA, his height is not only not a hindrance in Liverpool's playing ecosystem but an advantage. "You look for height and speed, and that's not easy. Centre-backs are becoming more and more physically complete," says Gerard Autet. "It's important that you master the aerial game. If you press high and well organised, your opponents often don't have the quality to come out short with the ball under control, so they'll just throw long. And with a long ball forward, the centre-back is more likely to win the duel".

In addition to factors arising from their own teams, such as the coach's idea of the game and the characteristics of the team-mates around them, the evolution in the defensive demands on centre-backs has also been stimulated by opponents. In particular, the rise of a type of striker who is different from the classic finisher, and who takes on a greater role in areas away from the penalty area. Without the clear and permanent reference of one or two strikers stuck in the centre of the attack, and replaced by much more mobile and versatile models, central defenders have had to adapt their behaviour to scenarios in which the threat to their area does not occur in a direct way. "The strikers of today have nothing to do with those of the past. Obviously, it's not the same as marking Messi playing as a false nine, who comes down, makes you get out of position, hesitates and then when he's dragged you out of the defensive line, he faces you and beats you", explains Autet.

Carlos Cuéllar, before retiring in 2019 played as a centre-back in the Spanish, Scottish, English and Israeli leagues, also mentioned this issue when analysing the current situation of the position with journalist Miguel Quintana: "Nowadays, the aim is to break the lines, to try to get a centre-back out of position to attack that space. It often happened to me that I had to play without the opposing striker's reference point. That's the most difficult thing for a defender. If you put a two-metre striker in front of me, I fight with him, I have no problem. But when you have to think about whether you go out or not, when if you go out, they attack your back... That's what you're looking for in today's football, and the characteristics of the strikers are very different. Shorter, quicker, more dynamic, who move well between the lines, who are able to get a defender out of the area and who can break into space"[158].

The coaches' new instructions for the defensive work of the centre-backs have not only been reflected in the matches but also in the training sessions. A different game entails a different preparation, providing the player with new tools that he must know how to use during the matches. The objectives of the training sessions change," comments Adrián Cervera, "because defensively you have to dominate other situations (...), if your team is pressing higher for longer periods, you tend to take time away from training defensive phases of more intermediate situations or retreat"[159].

In turn, as in the case of goalkeepers, the training of central defenders has had to adjust to a new paradigm in which fullbacks play a fundamental role with the ball at their feet. Their value in the ball out wide, their ability to generate the first advantage without losing the ball and to provide an outlet for the midfielders, has forced a reformulation of the type of preparation they receive, incorporating into their day-to-day work a content that in the past

---

158 Quintana, Miguel (7th November, 2019). How have centre-backs changed in the last 20 years? *¿Cómo han cambiado los centrales en los últimos 20 años?* | With Carlos Cuéllar. Extracted from: **https://youtu.be/xPz3ni5_Xfs**

159 *En un momento dado* (2021). Interview with Adrián Cervera. Extracted from: **https://eumd.es/2021/04/entrevista-adrian-cervera/**

was generally much more secondary. The central defender must be a fundamental part of the attacking play.

Marcelino Elena, who played as a centre-back in the 1990s for Sporting Gijón, Mallorca, Newcastle and the Spanish national team, pointed out in the pages of El País that "everything has been standardised and the ball is encouraged to come out from the centre-backs from a very early age (...). There are those who barely touch the ball with their heads until the age of 18"[160].

Paco Jémez also points in the direction of the change in methodology and content of the training sessions, to explain the evolution of both the game and the individual characteristics of centre-backs: "Every idea of the game has certain connotations, and these connotations entail a typology of player. In turn, that typology of player entails training to compete in that way. It's not that nowadays defenders are magically more technical than before. You work with them at a younger age to make them more technical, because you need them to be technical to do a specific job. If in ten years' time, direct play and counter-attacking play resurfaces, a style of play that prioritises not making mistakes in your defence and switching the ball away from your goal as quickly as possible, then, defenders like those of 15 or 20 years ago will start to emerge again".

The former head coach of UD Las Palmas, Rayo Vallecano, Granada and Cruz Azul in Mexico, among others, also underlines the importance of conviction when it comes to the central defender daring to take risks with the ball in order to support the team's ball delivery. "A player who is in the first division can't be bad. He may be more or less gifted, but he can't be bad. If he were, he wouldn't be playing first division football. So on that basis, all defenders can play the ball. Sometimes people think that playing

---

160 Cudeiro, Juan L. (2018). The death of the classic centre-back. *La muerte del central clásico. El País newspaper.*

the ball is about dribbling six times in the box or doing an overhead lob, but it's not. I don't ask my defenders to do that, I ask them to play football. I ask them to have good control and a good pass. That's all. That's playing the ball well for a centre-back. I've never asked a defender to dribble where he doesn't have to. What we work on is to have strong ball control, good passing, which is an important action in the game, to make a pass into space for a team-mate and have the confidence to switch the ball by breaking lines where the ball may travel and land to the feet, in front of the player".

A change of priorities due to the growing importance of the full-backs in their team's playmaking game has put the focus on the abilities of players on the ball to the detriment of other virtues more traditionally associated more to the position of centre-back. Little by little, full-backs have been moulded to the mandate of a style of football in which the importance of playing clean from the back, with a controlled build-up to advance with the ball in possession along with certain defensive attitudes closely related to the ball, have stamped their mark on the personality of a large number of teams. The centre-back is not a detached part of the attack, but a key player in it. A player capable of improving it and helping the offensive development of his team-mates and at the same time, a player who benefits from his team's play in the opposing half.

Based on this conception of the game, of the impact of the attack in defining defensive contexts, and of the role that the full-backs could play in it, the centre-backs came to incorporate as an indispensable requirement the ability to provide the team with a good outlet for the ball from the back. They were incorporated as decisive pieces in the game with the ball, understanding that as long as they contributed to the improvement of the attack, they would also facilitate the subsequent defensive reaction of the whole team. If you have the ball, your opponents don't and if they have it too far away from the goal, it's more diffi-

cult for them to score. "Johan Cruyff said that the most important players for a team to play well with the ball in their possession are their defenders. If you come out well, you can play well, if you don't, there is no option. Johan believes that what balances the game is the ball. Lose too many, and you're an unbalanced team. Lose a few, and you're all about balance", illustrated Pep Guardiola[161].

Guardiola, got first-hand experience of being part of the Dream Team that Johan Cruyff built at Barcelona, taking control of a midfield that played just ahead of a defender as unique as Ronald Koeman. The Dutchman, with a prodigious shot and a reading of the game carved out of midfield areas, was an emblem and one of the pillars of the team that brought the first European Cup to the Blaugrana's museum, taking on the role of organiser of play from a central position, normally more linked to defensive duties. "When the centre-back drove into midfield, it made me better. If the player marking me was going to defend, I was on my own. If my centre-back didn't drive forward, I didn't touch the ball"[162]. As a coach, then, Guardiola has sought that same essence in his centre-backs. Of Rafa Márquez, for example, the Catalan from Santpedor said that "there will only be one or two others who have that ability to make their team-mates better through passing and coming off the ball"[163].

Another former Barcelona player, Gabriel Milito, despite the fact that physical problems prevented him from continuing in Guardiola's team, recalled in the book "Che Pep" by Vicente Muglia, the importance given by the coach to the central defenders advancing the ball: "The coaches I had had in my career made a point of stressing to me that,

---

161 Guardiola, Josep (2006). Going out as a couple. *Salir de novios. El País newspaper.*

162 GOL (24th July, 2019). 90 minutes with Pep Guardiola. Extracted from: https://youtu.be/hNCjnwKEea4

163 Morén, Albert (2014). *En un momento dado*: So you are not forgotten. Extracted from: https://eumd.es/2014/08/para-que-no-te-olviden/

because of the position I occupied on the pitch, I didn't have to take risks. Gaby, control and pass', they would ask me. Some even explained to me that losing a ball in the area where I moved was very dangerous for the team. Ever since I was a kid I always liked to move forward, to carry the ball forward, but as a professional I never had enough freedom to do that, except in isolated plays. When Pep played for me at Barcelona, he opened up my head. In training I used to control and pass as I'd got used to doing over the years and one day, he grabbed me and said: "No, Gaby, you have to move the ball forward to the midfield"[164].

Márquez, Milito, Piqué, Puyol, Abidal or Mascherano in Barcelona; Boateng, Dante, Alaba or Kimmich in Munich; and Otamendi, Stones, Laporte or Ruben Dias in Manchester, as interpreters of a new role reserved for centre-backs. "I love guys like Stones. Because it's not easy to be a central defender with me. You have to defend 40 metres from your goal and come out and build the play. In other teams the centre-backs just have to get into their box to clear balls with their heads and play long (...). At City, a defender's mistakes make it obvious because they are very difficult to solve"[165].

"The change has been motivated by a requirement," says Jémez, "when they started to impose a more combinative style that sought to have possession of the ball and defend with the ball. It's a style in which everyone has to help (...). Before, what used to be the style was for coaches to ask for simplicity from the central defenders. Defenders were not allowed to make mistakes with the ball. In my time as a player, Juanma Lillo was the first one who started to ask us to have a certain cleanliness with the ball, to not always throw it straight up and to try to come out and play. Not in such a radical way as is often asked nowadays, but I

---

164 Muglia, Vicente (2016), *Che Pep*. Buenos Aires: Editorial Libro Fútbol.
165 Torres, Diego (2018). Guardiola is looking for a 'Puyol' in Laporte. *El País newspaper.*

remember him as one of the first who at that time started to ask defenders to come out and play. José Antonio Camacho, in the national team, also always asked us to be able to lend a hand in midfield. But we always gave priority to our defensive facet," recalls the Canary Islander coach.

Gerard Autet's memory is very similar: "Before, it was all about the centre-back defending well, being rigorous in marking and being able to give a direct ball to his striker. That was more than enough. Nowadays, however, most coaches ask you to have a clean start with the ball from the back (...). In professional football, the first coach who made me realise the importance of dividing with the ball to attract an opponent was Bernd Schuster. At Xerez we played with a five-man defence, and he always asked me to drive the ball into midfield. He insisted that I should be calm and that if I had to cross the centre of the pitch, I should do it without fear. That was in the second division, at a time when it wasn't very common for coaches to give you these assignments. I remember that period as one of the ones I enjoyed the most, because it was a type of game that suited me very well.

(...) Normally the coaches asked me to be more practical and to find the striker quickly with a long ball. We did it at Sporting with Manolo Preciado. If we could play out wide, we played out wide, but if we couldn't, we tried to be more direct and send the ball quickly to strikers like David Barral or Mate Bilić.

In order to get the centre-backs to take on responsibilities that were not theirs in the past, the coaches can count on the fact that after a decade of evolution, the new generation of full-backs now have close role models with whom they can identify. Where others once had the mirror of tough, specialist markers nullifying the opposing striker, today's young players look to centre-backs who give voice to the position through the ball with complete naturalness. Centre-backs whose teams demand that they play a leading role in attack, and who have the personality to incorporate the demand and carry it out without hesitation.

For example, Matthijs de Ligt, one of the most talented youngsters in the position of centre-back, recognises Gerard Piqué and Sergio Ramos as the role models he tries to be like, while Inter Milan centre-back Alessandro Bastoni identifies Thiago Silva as his idol because "he has everything: speed, technique, anticipation..."[166], Dayot Upamecano envies Ramos' personality[167], and Ronald Araújo envies Piqué building play into space from the back[168]. There are even those who place their references in positions more directly linked to attacking play, such as Brazilian Gabriel Magalhães, Arsenal centre-back who points to his compatriot Ronaldinho as his idol, or Sevilla's Jules Koundé, who praises players such as Karim Benzema and Sadio Mané: "It's curious that they are all attackers"[169].

The need for technical players with vision and personality to start the attack from the centre-back position has, in fact, led to coaches sometimes opting to readapt more attacking players to the position. It is a resource that Guardiola has used with relative assiduity, as demonstrated by the cases of Yaya Touré, Javier Mascherano, David Alaba, Javi Martínez, Kimmich and Fernandinho, whose move to defence Pep explained in the following terms: "I think Fernandinho can perform well in ten different positions,

166 Biondini, Chiara (2019). *Tutto Mercato Web*: Parma, Bastoni: "Bruno Alves is like a father, Thiago Silva is my idol". Extracted from: https://www.tuttomercatoweb.com/altre-notizie/parma-bastoni-bruno-alves-come-un-padre-thiago-silva-il-mio-idolo-1208224

167 *Culé Manía* (2020). Upamecano plays on both wings with Barça and Real Madrid. Extracted from: https://www.culemania.com/universo-blaugrana/upamecano-juega-dos-bandas-con-barca-real-madrid_339513_102.html

168 Martín, Eduardo (2021). *FCBarcelona Noticias*: Ronald Araújo confesses: His future, his idol, his aspirations at Barça.... Extracted from: https://www.fcbarcelonanoticias.com/jugadores/ronald-araujo-confiesa-futuro-idolo-aspiraciones-barcelona_264001_102.html

169 Espina, José A. (2020). Koundé: "¿Shorty? Cannavaro won a Ballon D'or". *AS newspaper.*

because he has the quality to play anywhere (...). He can play in defence because he is quick, aggressive, intelligent and has a good head. He has the quality to play the ball out from the back and pass forward"[170].

In keeping with his idea that "an intelligent midfielder can always play at centre-back", Javier Mascherano"[171], probably underwent the most paradigmatic transformation, both in terms of the productive nature of the change and its longevity. The fact is that the little boss played as Barça's centre-back for seven and a half seasons, and under the orders of five different coaches (Guardiola, Vilanova, Martino, Luis Enrique and Valverde), during a period in which the player himself came to express his preference for his new position: "At this club I feel more comfortable at centre-back than in midfield (...), the reality is that I feel more comfortable at Barcelona playing as a centre-back. Without the concepts that Pep gave me over the last year and a half, it would have been impossible for me to play at centre-back"[172].

During the 2013-14 season, Paco Jémez also created a centre-back capable of making the difference from a midfielder like Saúl Ñíguez. A conversion that earned the player the second most minutes for Rayo Vallecano that season, and which the coach remembers very positively: "Saúl is a player who can play in any position. He is the player that all coaches want because if you use him as a striker he does well, if you use him as a midfielder he does well, if you use him as a defender he does well, and I think that if you use him as a goalkeeper he would also do well. We used him a lot of times as a centre-back because he

---

170 Murphy, Darragh. *Sports Joe*: Pep Guardiola identifies player he can transform into Manchester City's answer to Javier Mascherano. Extracted from: https://www.sportsjoe.ie/football/pep-guardiola-identifies-player-he-can-transform-into-manchester-citys-answer-to-javier-mascherano-88809?cmpredirect

171 León, Rafael (2012). *Perarnau Magazine*: The centre-backs at Barça. Extracted from: https://www.martiperarnau.com/los-centrales-del-barca/

172 El Mundo (2012). "I feel much more comfortable as centre-back, thanks to Guardiola". *El Mundo*.

had spectacular physical abilities and because technically, he was better than the other options".

In addition to Saúl, since 2010 there have also been other examples such as Rodrigo Caio, Sven Bender, Jérémy Toulalan, Joel Matip, Hedwiges Maduro and Igor Zubeldia. Men who, from the defence and looking the action in the face, have added the technique and interpretation of the game typical of a midfielder, but who, situated in midfield, could find more obstacles.

Martí Perarnau draws on this last thread to describe the context that led Javi Martínez to go from being a midfielder under Jupp Heynckes to being a central defender for Guardiola. "When it came to destroying, Javi Martínez was very good at it. Like when he played in double pivot alongside Schweinsteiger at Bayern under Heynckes. But to build, as a positional midfielder, he didn't have the clarity of ideas or the technical speed to adapt. His conversion as a central midfielder was essential as he was a very useful player but using him in the right place. In fact as a centre-back he did not have a great outlet for the ball. What he did was pass the ball quickly to the full-back or the midfielder, but he had many other qualities that made him a very interesting defender. That's why Guardiola wanted him"[173], recalls the journalist.

The same centre of defence that once served some as a place to hide their lack of physical speed, now transformed into an ally to hide the difficulties of certain midfielders in keeping up with the ball circulation demanded by teams in midfield.

---

173 *En un momento dado* (2021). Interview with Martí Perarnau. Extracted from: https://eumd.es/2021/04/entrevista-marti-perarnau/

CHAPTER 6

THE MIDFIELD WITHOUT SURNAMES

> "Tell me which midfielder you play with and I'll tell you which team you are".
>
> JUANMA LILLO

Pep Guardiola's history on the bench at Fútbol Club Barcelona got off to an unexpected start. He started qualifying for the Champions League and then stumbled in the first rounds of the Spanish La Liga against two theoretically affordable rivals such as Numancia and Racing Santander. Adding the two matches together, the Blaugrana were only able to get one point, a meagre haul that did not prevent some early doubts about the team and the stance the club board had taken in choosing the coach to revive Barça after two seasons of disappointment.

Although the memory has often wanted to immortalise them as two sister games, as actors in the same chapter in the story of Guardiola's team, the truth is that for the Santpedor-born manager the only thing the two episodes had in common was an undesirable end result. After the defeat in Soria, Pep has been visibly dissatisfied with his team's performance ("we didn't respect the rules of positional play that we had played until now (...), everyone has an obligation, everyone has a job"[174]), but his diagnosis of the draw against Racing Santander at the Camp Nou was much more positive: "I have nothing to reproach for the game (...), the players are hurt, but my obligation is to encourage them, and I have to make them see that they have played and done well"[175].

Johan Cruyff must have thought similarly, and the following day he spoke of Barça's play in the following terms : "We need to polish the last pass —the most difficult one—, and we need to polish the decisive final touch. But I have no doubts (...), the way I see it, it looks very, very good"[176]. It is also said that Andrés Iniesta, who starred in both games, went to Guardiola's office to reassure the coach and dispel any doubts that the two bad results might be causing him: "Don't worry, coach, we're going to win everything. We are on the right track. Keep it up, OK? We're playing great, and we're enjoying training. Please don't change anything".[177]

What made the difference in Guardiola's eyes between the defeat against Numancia and the draw against Racing Santander was that in the first game the team had not stuck to the plan. They had not followed the instructions to put into practice what they had been working on during the previous weeks. Pep had failed to get the players to trust his ideas in the face of difficulty. This was a particularly delicate aspect, as the numerous innovations that the Santpedor-born manager was trying to introduce into the team's play, some of them ground-breaking and strange in the eyes of the group, needed the receptiveness of his players, and there was also the possibility that the lack of

---

174 Alonso, Paco (2008). "We don't respect rules". *Mundo Deportivo.*
175 Solé, Sergi (2008). Guardiola: "I am very happy". *Mundo Deportivo.*
176 El País (2008). Cruyff: "This Barça looks very, very good". *El País.*
177 Díaz-Agero, Alejandro (2016). The moment Iniesta changed Guardiola's career. *ABC.*

experience on the bench could compromise his authority when it came to convincing the players.

It was not in vain that one of his first announcements as head coach of the first team was the intention to dispense with three of the names that had led the previous project under Frank Rijkaard: Ronaldinho, Deco and Samuel Eto'o. His first objective was to persuade, to inject the squad with the conviction of a new way to do things, and without accrediting achievements as a coach at the highest level, doing so with the three of them could be more difficult than with the rest. "All styles are good. All of them. I will try to convince the players and all the people in the dressing room of the style I feel. I can't win without transmitting what I feel. I know that this is the way that can bring us closer to victory"[178].

His explicit dissatisfaction with the team's performance on the first matchday resulted, a week later, with Pedro Rodríguez and Sergio Busquets in the starting line-up, two already convinced pupils. Two young players who had already been instructed and familiarised with his playing philosophy, and who had already put it into practice under his orders in the reserve team during the previous season. A 21-year-old winger, responsible, obedient, and hard-working, and the 20-year-old midfielder to whom Guardiola had entrusted the position that, after a life as a footballer devoted to it, he knew more and more and what was best.

He is technically superior to Touré and Keita," Cruyff wrote of the midfielder's league debut, "positionally, he looks like a veteran. With and without the ball. With the ball, he made easy what was difficult: one/two touches. Without the ball, another masterclass: to be in the right place to intercept and recover by running just enough. And he was young and inexperienced. The same sins as his

---

178 DeportesLD (27th April, 2012). Guardiola's presentation at Barcelona. Extracted from: https://www.youtube.com/watch?v=TYPpvRP78qE

coach. Sergio Busquets would end up taking over from Yaya Touré as the team's midfielder. Not that first season, as the Ivorian remained in charge of the position until injuries in defence led Guardiola to use him as a fullback, but from the following seasons onwards, he did.

Touré had arrived at the Camp Nou a year earlier to occupy the position that, until then, in Frank Rijkaard's project had alternated between Rafa Márquez, José Edmílson and Thiago Motta. Like them, Yaya Touré would be the player who, positioned in front of the centre-back pairing, would act as the link between the defensive line and the midfield. Of the three midfielders, he would be the one who would play in a more withdrawn position and mainly in a holding role, despite the fact that previously at Olympiakos and later at Manchester City he had demonstrated some enormously powerful attacking skills. The technique, route, and overwhelming physical ability that in other latitudes made him an unstoppable finisher from the second line, in the Barça side of Xavi, Deco and Andrés Iniesta made him the bodyguard of the more creative midfielders.

Both the role and the distribution corresponded to the standards of the time, for in the early 2000s in top-level football an interpretation of balance based on counterbalance games reigned supreme. One in which the distribution of tasks was clearly compartmentalised and in which the block was formed from the sum of different profiles. Thus, if a full-back stood out for having a more attacking attitude, his counterpart on the opposite flank embodied a more defensive and less joyful figure in attack. The same logic was reproduced in midfield, with players oriented towards creativity on the ball accompanied by obedient and self-sacrificing squires. Each covered a spectrum of the game, and so, between them, they covered everything.

So much so that, during those years, "defensive" was the surname that naturally incorporated the position of midfielder, as if the attitude of its occupant defined the position as much as its location on the pitch. As if goalkeepers were no longer called that and were renamed offensive goalkeepers for their active participation in the construction of play, or as if wingers were given the epithet "defensive" for their increasing involvement in pressing. The midfield of the teams, then, distinguished two worlds: that of the midfielders in charge of attacking and that of the midfielders in charge of defending. It was not for nothing that in those years it was common to see players with a background as central defenders playing in the midfield.

"Players like me have become extinct," lamented Pep Guardiola in 2004. "I haven't changed, my skills haven't diminished. It's just that football is different now. It's played at a faster pace and is much more physical. The tactics are different. You have to be a ball-winner, a player who goes out onto the pitch to steal the ball. Like Patrick Vieira or Edgar Davids. If you can also pass the ball that's fine, it's an advantage, but the emphasis, as far as midfielders are concerned, is all on defensive"[179].

An emblematic case of this commitment to balance based on the sum of opposites was Real Madrid between 1999 and 2003. Real Madrid had some of the best players in the world in their eleven: Zinedine Zidane, Ronaldo Nazario, Roberto Carlos, Raúl González, and Luis Figo. The so-called "Galácticos" formed a constellation of stars with a wealth of individual attacking talent that was difficult to match. Such a large number of attacking players, as well as the freedom with which they were integrated into the team's play, however, required a figure in charge of compensating the tactical structure. Claude Makélélé, once a midfielder with the ability to come in from the second line, became the reverse side of the plethora of talented attackers who were part of Madrid's approach to the game. He was the defensive specialist in midfield who, often positioned behind all the stars, based his importance for the team on the difference. He was not just one more

---

179 Marcotti, Gabriele (2004). Coping with a lack of pep. *The Times*.

player, but one different from the rest, which allowed him to have an impact on tasks that nobody else was attending to. In a team where full-backs, forwards and the rest of the midfielders were attack-oriented, Claude defended for everyone.

Esta This idea of balance between opponents was even repeated in exceptional cases such as Andrea Pirlo. The Italian was a former playmaker (trequartista) rediscovered as a midfielder (regista), with a great influence on his teams' attacking performance but little ability without the ball. Carlo Mazzone, coach of Brescia during the 2000-2001 season, had sensed the change that Carlo Ancelotti would consolidate in Milan[180]. "As a 'trequartista', the lack of space could nullify his skills, but as a creative midfielder his contribution increased," explained Mazzone[181].

During his playing days, Ancelotti had seen Agostino Di Bartolomei successfully complete the same transformation, when they both joined AS Roma under Swedish coach Nils Liedholm[182], and he did not hesitate to hand Pirlo the keys to Milan's midfield from the pivot position: "I had the immense good fortune to meet Ancelotti at Milan. It was a before and after in my career. I stopped playing as a midfielder and started playing as an organiser. That's where my real career began (...). He is my footballing father (...). Until Ancelotti made me play in front of the defence, that position in Italy was only occupied by defensive players with the same idea: to destroy rather than build. It was only when I started to play as a pivot that the trend changed. It showed that it was possible to win by

180 Giner, J. y Beltran, M. (2017). *Panenka*: 7 moments of "pure Pirlo »: thus the myth was built. Extracted from: https://www.panenka.org/pasaportes/7-momentos-de-puro-andrea-pirlo-asi-se-construyo-el-mito/

181 Murray, Andrew (2017). *Four Four Two*: Andrea Pirlo | "I knew I was better than the rest from very young". Recuperado de: https://www.fourfourtwo.es/noticias-y-cu-riosidades/entrevistas/andrea-pirlo-desde-muy-joven-supe-que-era-mejor-que-los-demas_27051_102.html

182 Rojas, Abel (2010). *Ecos del balón*: "The eighth king of Rome" and "the baron". "*L'ottavo re di Roma" e "il Barone*". Extracted from: http://www.ecosdelbalon.com/2010/10/l%C2%B4ottavo-re-di-roma-e-il-barone_/

playing good football. I'm proud to have instilled the 'jogo bonito' in Italy"[183]. Ancelotti's balancing act, in this case, translated into the choice of expert playmakers such as Gennaro Gattuso or Massimo Ambrosini to accompany Pirlo's attacking talent.

It is not surprising, therefore, that while this was happening in the teams that most commonly played with a single midfielder, a new trend was spreading to countless corners of planet football: the double pivot. This was a form of organisation in which two players shared the most rearward area of the midfield, and in which, therefore, the distribution of both space and tasks between the two was very marked.

Sergio González Soriano, who shaped them as a player at Espanyol, Deportivo La Coruña and the Spanish national team, analysed how they worked as coach of Real Valladolid: "One of the rules that the two pivots must comply with is not to overlap. Both offensively and defensively, they must not cross the imaginary line that divides the pitch vertically (...). You have a slightly more defensive profile, with good feet but above all legs, running coverage and a lot of reading of the game. This player is complemented very well by another player, who also have to have legs, but whose role is a little more to have the ball and try to combine and develop (...) Ideally, they should be a little bit staggered. The pivot with a more defensive profile a little further forward, with the possibility of joining the attack and getting to the finishing areas"[184].

Since the French national team won the 1998 World Cup with Deschamps and Petit playing behind the midfielders, and the Euro 2000 with Patrick Vieira alongside Deschamps as a support for Zidane, Djorkaeff or Thierry

---

183 Cañizares, Rubén (2015). Interview: "Pirlo is here to stay". "*Hay Pirlo para rato*". *ABC*.

184 *Diario As* (17th December, 2019). Sergio González explains the functions of the double pivot in the 4-4-2 | *Futbología* #8. Extracted from: **https://youtu.be/O_IIbkYg-Gel**

Henry, the idea of reinforcing the midfield with two players positioned just in front of the centre-backs quickly became a school of thought. Formulas such as the 1-4-2-3-1 or 1-4-4-2-2 made their mark. The 2003-2004 season was particularly representative of this new trend. That season, Rafa Benítez's Valencia won the Spanish league and the UEFA Cup with the double pivot of David Albelda and Rubén Baraja becoming the emblem. In England, Arsène Wenger's Arsenal won the Premier League without defeat, led by an unstoppable Thierry Henry and relying on the solidity provided by the midfield pairing of Patrick Vieira and Gilberto Silva. To cap it all off, the Champions League went to a surprising Porto side then coached by a young José Mourinho, with Deco as the star player and the Costinha-Maniche tandem at the heart of their competitive squad.

"At Liverpool, with Rafa Benítez, we normally played a 1-4-2-3-1 formation and I used to play as a left pivot. My game had to adapt a bit to the characteristics of the other pivot," recalls Alonso. "If my partner was a player like Steven Gerrard, I had to have a more positional role because he would go further up the pitch. On the other hand, when I played alongside a player like Mascherano in recent years, he was less attacking and I had to play a bit further forward to get closer and connect with Gerrard and Fernando Torres."[185] If, as the quote attributed to Juanma Lillo says, "tell me which midfielder you play with and I'll tell you which team you are"[186], midfielders at the turn of the century, epitomised like no other position a way of understanding the balance of teams based on the sum of opposing characteristics. In midfield, as a general rule, there were no shared tasks.

---

185 The Coaches' Voice (29th May, 2019). Xabi Alonso: My Role At Liverpool, Real Madrid & Bayern Munich - Masterclass. Extracted from: https://youtu.be/8OcXUJ2M-7gA

186 Quintana, Miguel (2018). *Panenka*: Being a midfielder in Spain. Extracted from: https://www.panenka.org/pasaportes/ser-mediocentro-en-espana/

"In the end, it was all about sharing the workload," says Luis Milla, a Barça youth player in whom Cruyff discovered the first midfielder of the "Dream Team" back in the summer of 1988[187]. Under the Dutchman, Milla played as an organiser of Barcelona's style of play for two seasons, before leaving for Real Madrid, leaving free space in the team that Pep Guardiola would make his own for a decade. Away from the Camp Nou and the 4 that Cruyff had defined as the sole midfielder in his system, Milla would find himself back in the double pivot. He had known it in Barça's youth ranks, having paired with Guillermo Amor, before Cruyff's arrival introduced the 1-3-4-3, and he would put it into practice again at both Real Madrid and Valencia:

"Playing alone I was very comfortable, but I have also adapted to playing with a double pivot. With Ranieri, Cúper or Capello we played with two midfielders (...). It's a formula with which you want to be stronger and occupy more space in the middle (...). The normal thing when you play with two midfielders is that one is more defensive and the other more offensive. It was like that at Barça B when I played alongside Amor, or with Baraja or Farinós at Valencia, who were more attacking players who could play more attacking football. With them I had to be in charge of keeping the position a bit more. (...) At Real Madrid there was also a time when Fernando Hierro and I played as midfielders. I stayed back, and in those years Hierro scored a lot of goals. He was a player with a lot of pace, capable of coming in from the second line, he had a shot from outside the box... he was even the team's top scorer one season"[188].

Another midfielder brought up in La Masía, Sergi Samper, had a different experience away from the Camp Nou

---

187 Morén, Albert (2016). *En un momento dado*: That first summer in Papendal. Extracted from: **https://eumd.es/2016/01/primer-verano-johan-cruyff-barcelona/**
188 *En un momento dado* (2021). Interview with Luis Milla. Extracted from: **https://eumd.es/2021/04/entrevista-luis-milla/**

to Milla in relation to the double pivot. The Catalan, the first player to reach the Barça first team, having started out in the FCB Escola at just six years of age, moulded his game in the youth ranks already completely influenced by the model that Cruyff imported to Barcelona. When he left the club, therefore, a new world awaited him: "At Granada, with Lucas Alcaraz, we always used the double pivot. I had never played like that (...). For me, midfield play changes a lot. Above all, it depends on how the two pivots are positioned, whether they play at different heights or not. I grew up at Barça and I'd been playing all my life as the only midfielder, when I started playing as a double pivot, I was a bit lost. I didn't know how to position myself, how to measure the distances between the pivots... it took me a while until I was able to adapt"[189].

The rise and consolidation of Sergio Busquets in Guardiola's Barça marked the beginning of a new era[190]. "Everyone is a participant. I don't understand football as a sport in which some players only defend and others only attack", Pep Guardiola exclaimed at his presentation as Barça coach, while the attention of the football world was focused on the European Championship in Austria and Switzerland. While Pep was planning the start of his successful project, the Spanish national team would win the title after a 44-year drought, under the leadership of Luis Aragonés and a midfield capable of bringing together Xavi, Iniesta, David Silva and Cesc Fàbregas on the pitch at the same time. Just behind them, one of the keys to success was the Spanish-Brazilian Marcos Senna, a pillar in Manuel Pellegrini's close-knit Villarreal, and a midfielder who, far from compensating for the accumulation of creative profiles in the midfield of the national team by orienting his performance towards strictly defensive duties, was in-

---

189 *En un momento dado* (2021). Interview with Sergi Samper. Extracted from: https://eumd.es/2021/04/entrevista-sergi-samper/

190 Marcet. Intelligent Football: This is the midfielder of the future. Extracted from: https://marcetfootball.com/es/mediocentro-del-futuro/

tegrated with them as one more. He would do so, as Oscar Cano analyses in *"El modelo de juego del Fútbol Club Barcelona"*(The model of play of FC Barcelona), "without injecting controversy", since, as the coach describes, "the greater the similarity, the easier it is to establish interactions"[191].

The same idea was developed by Jorge Valdano in an interview with Orfeo Suárez with newspaper *El Mundo*, where the Argentinian celebrated the fact that Luis Aragonés had avoided "that theory of putting one player who unbalances and another who recovers, because in the end you don't do either one or the other. He gave up centimetres and opted for players with similar characteristics, with complicities that turned Spain into an indecipherable team. And the fact is that if Iniesta gives it to a specialist in destruction, the ball doesn't come back. Therefore, it is a lie that the game is shared, it is not shared at all"[192].

Attacking and defending, as well as two connected moments of the game, would be shared tasks. "We will attack better if we defend well, and we will defend better if we attack well", Pep Guardiola proclaimed before his Barça had even started on the road, anticipating an idea of play in which balance is not provided by the sum of different players, but of equals. Attacking and defending as a single unit.

In this concept of balance, as opposed to the one that a few years earlier had chiselled double pivots and defensive midfielders, Sergio Busquets embodied many of the issues that would henceforth define a new type of midfielder. A midfielder, now without a surname, fused with the game in each and every phase of the game. "He had in his favour that he knew what Pep wanted. On a tactical

---

191 Cano, Oscar (2009). The *model of play at FC Barcelona. A network of meaning interpreted from the paradigm of complexity.* España: MCSports.

192 Suárez, Orfeo (2008). Valdano: "Intelligence is suspicious and Guardiola represents that". *"La inteligencia es sospechosa y Guardiola la representa".* El Mundo.

level and on a game level. That made it a bit easier for me"[193].

One of the most important aspects of the job that Guardiola reserved for his midfielders had to do with starting the game from the back. With the collaboration so that the ball came out cleanly from the start. It was a nuclear moment to facilitate the work of the forwards and the rest of the midfielders, and to make possible an advance with the lines together in which, as a rule, the midfielder should be involved. With reading and technique when it comes to passing and the ability to get behind the strikers to receive behind the opposition's first line of pressure.

The abandonment of direct play and the commitment to a controlled start from defence, therefore, replaced a scenario in which teams often bypassed the pivots to get forward. One in which, by linking the defence directly with the forwards, the midfield would start to play from the rebound or the second play without having to receive from the back. The new path, on the other hand, required them to be accustomed to turning and orienting their bodies to connect defence and attack with the ball at grass level. New demands on the position which, for those less prepared to adapt to the new times, meant a relocation to other areas of the pitch, mainly in defence.

As such, Yaya Touré played the Copa del Rey and Champions League finals of 2009, or the semi-final duels against Inter Milan that would deprive Barça of playing the 2010 final in Madrid. Martí Perarnau also recalls how Javi Martínez recovered the status of centre-back with Guardiola that Marcelo Bielsa had discovered for him a few years earlier in Bilbao. Just before Pep's arrival in Munich, the Navarrese had won a treble at Bayern, paired with Bastian Schweinsteiger in the Bavarian midfield, but Guardiola's

---

193 *Universo Valdano* (2018). "Sergio Busquets". Movistar +

approach to the single pivot position made it difficult for him to fit into the centre of the pitch[194].

Just like the case of Javi Martínez, for Javier Mascherano, leaving the double pivot also meant rediscovering himself as a centre-back under Guardiola. "The first few months at Barcelona were difficult for me," the little boss recalled on the Team Barça podcast. "I had to get used to positional play, to possession... to get involved in the construction of the game, which was something that in previous years I had become detached from. Until then, my role was to be the defensive midfielder and I stood out when the team didn't have the ball. But not when they did. When I arrived at Barça, Guardiola told me at every training session: here, everyone is involved in the construction of the game"[195].

"I was a defensive midfielder who was taught to steal, try to participate in the destruction of the game and, when it came to building, always be aware of where the team was unbalanced to try to cover the spaces", he admitted to Libero magazine in 2017. "At Barça it's the opposite (...), here a defensive pivot has to be part of the formation of the game. It's a concept that I'd never come across before and it was very difficult for me to adapt it"[196].

Paralelamente, At the same time, the era of defensive midfielders had shifted players who were used to playing in front of the defence but were not given the chance to play in a double pivot to inside positions. These were bad times for Cruyff's 4, and only Andrea Pirlo had managed to emerge unscathed from the new wave. Xavi Hernández, Guardiola's heir as the standard-bearer of the Dutch

---

194 *En un momento dado* (2021). Interview with Martí Perarnau. Extracted from: https://eumd.es/2021/04/entrevista-marti-perarnau/

195 *Team Barça Podcast* (2020, 9th October). Interview with Javier Mascherano. Extracted from: https://youtu.be/JNoUmkEAcjM

196 Cappa, María (2018). *Líbero*: Mascherano: "The idea at Barça is non-negotiable". "*En el Barça la idea es innegociable*". Extracted from: https://revistalibero.com/blogs/contenidos/mascherano-en-el-barca-la-idea-es-innegociable

model at Barça, was the player who responded best to the change. From a midfielder under Louis van Gaal, Llorenç Serra Ferrer and Carles Rexach, to an inside midfielder under Radomir Antić, Frank Rijkaard and Guardiola.

"At that time they tended to strengthen the midfield by bringing in players like Yaya Touré, with good feet and good ball handling, but more physical," examines Luis Milla. "Maybe what they understood is that Xavi could do more damage playing higher up. Being a midfielder who could start from the back perfectly, he could also play between the lines and know what to do in tight spaces".

The epicentre of the *Culé* game since Pep's arrival on the bench, the successes of Barça and the Spanish national team and his impact and influence on the way both teams functioned multiplied the search for similar profiles in all corners of the planet. The recipe for success was Barça's formula, and this involved a midfielder like the one from Terrassa.

The first temptation was to copy identical profiles without success, as there was not another Xavi, nor another Iniesta, another Messi, another Busquets, or another Dani Alves to combine with him to achieve the same effect. Players are themselves and their relationships with others, and if it was already impossible to find two identical players, it was even more impossible to copy all eleven. But from the seed of that search an intention was born, the result of which a type of midfielder with certain characteristics common to Xavi Hernández was established in the elite. Very participative inside players, responsible for managing and directing their teams' play on the ball, who moved up a few metres, tasks that before the double pivots and defensive midfielders had been carried out by men like Guardiola or Fernando Redondo from the centre circle.

Like Xavi, Cesc Fàbregas, Marco Verratti, Ilkay Gündogan, Koke Resurrección, Ever Banega, Miralem Pjanić, Thiago Alcántara, Ander Herrera, Toni Kroos or Arthur

Melo was, have been or are those midfielders but from the inside. Alongside them, there are midfielders like Sergio Busquets, Thiago Motta, Alex Song, Julian Weigl, Bruno Soriano, Ander Iturraspe, Rodri Hernández, Casemiro and Joshua Kimmich, adapted to the new times and the type of midfielders that accompany them. It was not for nothing that Xavi and Busquets followed opposite paths. The Terrassa native took what he learnt from the 4 at La Masía from midfield to inside, while Sergio turned his training as an inside player into a guide for his career as a midfielder: "When I arrived at Barça I was more of an inside midfielder. After that, I played as a midfielder on occasion, but very little, alternating between pivot and inside. Until I came to Barça B with Guardiola"[197].

Generous pivots ceding command and space to those who, originally, commanded their position. Partners of midfielders who like to appear in back positions to receive the ball directly from the defence, without intermediaries, momentarily occupying the place on the pitch that once belonged to them, without their current owners preventing them from travelling. Midfielders capable of abandoning their position when called upon by the interior to direct play from the centre circle. Kroos is one of the most important players in the team," says Casemiro, "he controls how the ball goes and at what pace we play: if Toni wants the team to go slower, the team goes slower; if he wants the team to go faster, the team goes faster. We play according to Toni Kroos"[198].

In addition to his close and harmonious coexistence with an inside midfielder who plays a key role in managing the game, Real Madrid's Brazilian midfielder represents like few others another of the characteristics that have come to define midfielders: the relationship with the off-the-

---

197 *Universo Valdano* (2018). "Sergio Busquets". Movistar +
198 Cuesta, Jorge (2020). *Mi Bundesliga*: "We play around Toni Kroos". "*Nosotros jugamos en función de Toni Kroos*". Casemiro. Extracted from: https://mibundesliga.com/nosotros-jugamos-en-funcion-de-toni-kroos-casemiro/

ball phases of their teams. Having generally moved away from a division of teams into blocks, in which some players were primarily oriented towards defence and others towards attack, and in which the midfielder was charged with compensating for the licences allowed to his more creative partners, the defensive role of the midfielders has gradually moved towards the configuration of a homogeneous block. In the same way that attacking is already everyone's job, and that is why positions such as goalkeeper, centre backs and midfielders have been forced to perfect their performance and ball handling, defending is also a shared task.

With this objective in mind, first pressing after a loss and then pressing against the opposition's attacking play have become defining features of most teams and, by extension, of the era in which they compete. It represents the umbrella under which to anchor stretches without the ball close to those previously developed with the ball, avoiding physically demanding defensive returns or the need to split the team into two halves. Defend as high up as possible and reduce the field as much as possible, in order to involve the team's most attacking players in the task.

Responding to the loss of the ball by running forward, moving forward and reducing the space between players. Wanting to defend and steal the ball away from the box. With the midfielders marking the border of the pressure and caging the opposition in their own half, forgetting the importance that at the beginning of the century was reserved for them by embedding themselves between the centre-backs to defend the area.

"Sergio Busquets is probably the player who understands and reads his position best when the opposition win the ball back," said Quique Setién after his debut match as Barça coach. "He knows very well and has it in his head to go forward to steal the ball, and the only thing we can do with respect to the rest of the players is to coordinate well so as not to leave spaces, because this is a mechanism that everyone has to do well and has to coordinate with the rest of the teammates who go forward to steal the ball"[199].

Nevertheless as in everything else, the influence of Guardiola's Barça's successes on other teams followed a twofold path: that of contagion and that of response. Thus, while some aspects of the Catalan's style book were gradually incorporated into the discourse of his rivals, at the same time, proposals emerged that were more oriented towards confrontation than assimilation. Since 2015 or so, one of them, forward pressing, has been a major player in top-level competition, and sets the tone for a reshaped scenario to which coaches and players are having to adapt.

In the specific case of the midfielders, they are adjusting to the harassment and reduction of space with which the players in front of them used to coexist. As a rule, the pivots were allowed to receive with space, in an area of the pitch seen as an aid for the inside players when the distances between the opposition's lines were restricted. However, the desire to press higher and higher up the pitch in search of recovery has led to the retraction at all levels of the midfield. Luis Milla, who since 2006 has coached Getafe, Lugo, Zaragoza and Abu Dhabi, and has been in charge of the Spanish Under-21s and the Indonesian national team, compares the football he experienced as a player with what he now observes from the bench: "Before, 75 or 80% of the time, when you played against a less powerful team, what the opposition did was to retreat and wait in their own half to come out quickly and surprise you. Not now. Now things have changed.

Receiving from behind, with little space and the close presence of an opponent has become a routine that, in

---

199 Morén, Albert (2020). *En un momento dado*: Two clues and a challenge for Setién on his debut. *Dos pistas y un reto en el debut de Setién*. Extracted from: https://eumd.es/2020/01/analisis-debut-quique-setien-barcelona-granada-messi-sergi-roberto-busquets-greizmann/#

midfield, is no longer exclusive to the inside midfielders. Midfielders also have to face this, requiring the incorporation into their game of conditions such as turning with the ball when the pass is received from behind, oriented control or a positioning of the body that facilitates continuity between the defence and the most advanced area of the midfield.

This is confirmed by Àlex Delmàs, who asserts that as a result of the rise of forward pressing "midfielders are either receiving more with their backs to the ball or they are receiving in more distant situations. What is clear is that it is more difficult to receive in pure midfield areas unless the games are very tight. Receiving in the midfield position cleanly, that doesn't happen anymore. At least in the first movement"[200].

Ander Herrera knows first-hand the particularities of each midfield zone. From midfield under Marcelo Bielsa to midfield under Ernesto Valverde and midfield when Mourinho took over at Manchester United, his career has given him different roles in the midfield of his teams: "I've often been asked which position I prefer to play in, whether as a number 10, number 8 or number 6. Whether as a number 10, number 8 or number 6. I say that it often depends on the opponent. Against an opponent who is totally closed in at the back, it's difficult to be the number 10 because the spaces are reduced and it's difficult to find your place. As a number 6 you have more chances. On the other hand, when you play against a team that is more open, more courageous and plays more one-on-one, the number 10 can enjoy more space"[201].

Ander was the regular midfielder for Manchester United that won the Red Devils' last European title, the UEFA Eu-

---

200 *En un momento dado* (2021). Interview with Àlex Delmàs. Extracted from: https://eumd.es/2021/04/entrevista-alex-delmas/

201 *En un momento dado* (2021). Interview with Ander Herrera. Extracted from: https://eumd.es/2021/04/entrevista-ander-herrera/

ropa League, which the side then managed by José Mourinho lifted after beating Ajax Amsterdam in the final. With Mkhitaryan and Juan Mata on the wings and Fellaini and Pogba on the inside, Mou chose Herrera to occupy the pivot position that season: "It was a year in which I mainly tried to improve my understanding of the game. When to give a pass between the lines taking a bit of a risk, or when to add passes with your centre-backs because the team needs it (...). A number 6 doesn't have the same demands as a number 10. As a playmaker, you can take losses and risks that you can't take as a midfielder".

It was 2017, and the impact of the rise of forward pressing forced the pivots to incorporate new resources into their game. "The pass from the goalkeeper to the midfielder with his back to him is seen in practically every game. Except for certain teams that never do it, like Getafe", confirms Ander. "I remember that Marcelino didn't like that pass to the midfielder with his back to the midfielder either, and he always wanted to use the two strikers to set up both the wide men and the midfielders (...). You have to get more and more used to that. There are more risks (...). Sergio Busquets often receives with his back to him, and he's perhaps the best in the world at that job. Or Marco Verratti, who I also love because he receives from the back and it looks like he's received from the front. He immediately turns to face the ball and starts to play.

This new scenario of fierce pressure on the midfield, in an area of the pitch where mistakes and losing the ball are severely punished, has opened up two broad paths in the evolution of the position. The first one has deepened the loneliness of its protagonists, wanting to take advantage of the spaces at the back of the pressure with two very advanced interiors. Practically two midfielders, between the defence and the opposing midfield, waiting for the pass to attack with metres in front of them and many opponents behind them.

"I think it's always best to move wide," said Àlex Delmàs. "The best thing is to make the pitch big when you come out from the back. Give air from the wide players, because in the end if you make the passing line close you can be an immediate help, but you end up generating a density of players that can be a problem. You end up having your team-mate close to you but also his marker".

A productive solitude for the midfielder if he manages to get the ball to them, but to do so successfully and without penitence, he has to carry a heavy load on his shoulders. The passing distance is lengthened, because on the one hand the opponent's pressure pushes the midfielder back and on the other hand the teammates in midfield tend to go forward. To become more and more forward.

Sergi Samper, who had his best season with Barça B as a midfielder in a team that used both inside midfielders in a very deep position, knows this well. Both Javi Espinosa and Edu Bedia were installed in the midfield of the reserve team then coached by Eusebio Sacristán, waiting for a pass from Samper to find them at the back of the opposing midfield: "It was a great season and I enjoyed it a lot. Eusebio liked to have the two inside players very high up (...). It has good things and not so good things. Sometimes I missed that one of the inside players was closer because it seemed to me that he had to pass a lot of metres (...). It is more and more difficult to find these passing lines because the teams are better organised. They cover these passes better on the inside and let them play more on the outside. But when you can jump a line is when the team breathes and has the ability to play in the opposition half".

Probably because of what Samper says, driving has gained weight in the range of options for a good number of midfielders. It works as a measure that serves both to move the pivot forward, bringing him closer to the inside players, and to challenge one of the opposing midfielders to abandon the position and leave a player free. "High pressing is changing what is asked of midfielders. Knowing how to get out of pressure when your back is turned, having the ability to dribble and drive... I think that profile of player is already establishing itself in the teams", assured Adrián Cervera[202].

An example of this is Rodri Hernández, the man chosen by Guardiola to take over from Fernandinho in the centre circle at Manchester City, who in an interview in the newspaper El País acknowledged that: "The way football has evolved I don't think you can play the same way you did seven years ago, because teams defend better and are more organised. (...). Driving is a facet that I didn't have internalised as a midfielder before, before it was more about receiving, passing, receiving, passing? based on the fact that the less you have the ball, the more speed you have. But Pep demands that you drive to attract opponents, fix them, and then divide with the pass. Before, I didn't see that as necessary for a pivot"[203].

Another case with some similarities is that of Frenkie de Jong. The Dutchman, before taking over the keys to Ajax Amsterdam's midfield, found his niche in Ten Haag's team as a left centre-back. "Most of the times I saw him, he played as a second centre-back next to De Ligt and when he got the ball, he would go over the lines with his dribbling", Pepe Serer, a member of the Barça scouting team that followed the player before he joined Ajax, also told newspaper El País[204].

One of De Jong's teammates at the Camp Nou, Antoine Griezmann, played against him twice for France in the UEFA Nations League, before they shared a dressing room. With Frenkie in midfield in the Dutch national team, Griezmann

---

202 *En un momento dado* (2021). Interview with Adrián Cervera. Extracted from: https://eumd.es/2021/04/entrevista-adrian-cervera/

203 Moñino, Ladislao (2019). Rodrigo: "At City, I finish the matches dead." "*En el City acabo los partidos muerto*". *El País*.

204 Quixano, Jordi (2020). Frenkie looks for De Jong. *Frenkie busca a De Jong. El País*.

recalled how, when he joined Barça how "in the game we played together I tried to press him as much as I could, but I never succeeded"[205]. "For a forward, going to press him is always difficult because he comes out of very complicated situations. He not only wins the field with a pass, but also by driving the ball and that's something unbelievable"[206].

The fact that the area to be managed by the midfielder is larger has also affected certain defensive functions of the teams that have opted to move the position of both inside midfielders forward. Variants such as the use of the full-backs in central areas, in order to provide the pivot with the shelter that at times the inside midfielders to have a greater physical range to go into the empty spaces when the team loses the ball, mark some of the new singularities of the position. "You're not going to defend less because you play differently. I don't know if I ran more at Atlético or now, but the feeling is that with City I finish games dead", Rodri Hernández said a few months after arriving at the Etihad Stadium[207].

For other teams, however, the response to the development of forward pressing and its impact on the comfort of the midfielders has been the opposite. Instead of moving the inside midfielders further back with the intention of occupying the space available behind the pressure, instead of moving them closer to provide an aid to the pivot who can reduce the chances of losing the ball. Even the teams that most commonly opt for the first of the two solutions, alternate with this second variant in certain matches or at certain times. "We are going to start to see more midfields with two players at the base", says Adrián Cervera, as he believes that when the opposition use individual man-to-

---

205 Mundo Deportivo (2019). Griezmann: "De Jong is the best player I have faced". *"De Jong es el mejor jugador al que me he enfrentado"*. *Mundo Deportivo*.

206 Martínez, Ferran (2019). Griezmann: "It will be easy to play alongside Messi". *"Será fácil jugar con Messi"*. *Mundo Deportivo*.

207 Moñino, Ladislao (2019). Rodrigo: "At City, I finish the matches dead". *"En el City acabo los partidos muerto"*. *El País newspaper*.

man pressure, as has become popular for some time now, "in the intervention zones, the ones closest to the ball holder, you don't need them to stretch you out but to help you, because the opposition bite you".

Movements catching up to the interior midfielders sometimes lead to a return to organisations with the appearance of a double pivot[208]. With the presence of a second player in the first level of the midfield, just in front of the defence, as the recipe for generating a close, short and simple passing option that makes it difficult for the opposition to recover forward. Also as a decoy to lure an opponent and oxygenate the midfield area. Or to find a defensive reinforcement when it comes to stopping the multitude of threats that the opponent can place between the lines when the team presses: inside players who climb up to the midfield, wingers with a tendency to come inside or centre forwards who like to influence outside the box.

In Sergi Samper's view on this issue, there may in fact be a link between the more widespread use of driving by midfielders and the recovery of double pivot structures. "Players who have this ability to drive the ball I think they should exploit it because it is a very good solution. Being able to break the opposition's lines helps the team a lot", the midfielder added. On the other hand, however, running up and down the pitch with the ball at their feet makes it difficult to maintain the positional order so often required in the midfield. "That's why, normally, these players who drive a lot and like to get into the box are much more comfortable playing with a double pivot", Samper continues. "Guardiola had always heard him say that he didn't trust a midfielder who was a box-to-box player[209] and who got into the box a lot".

---

208 Cervera, Adrián (2020), The approach game. *El juego de aproximación*. España.

209 A term used to describe midfielders with a long range of movement, who are able to go from one area to the other frequently.

Perhaps the most symptomatic case in this respect is that of Guardiola himself, when he has used Ilkay Gündogan or Bernardo Silva close to Rodri Hernández's position. Pep has even, from time to time, used a clearer second pivot such as Fernandinho alongside the Spanish international in his midfield. "When Rodri arrived in England perhaps he needed a bit of help, and a player with more experience in the Premier League like Gündoğan could lend him a hand," says Martí Perarnau of the pairing that Rodri and the German have sometimes formed behind a more advanced De Bruyne.

The Santpedor native's two former clubs, FC Barcelona and Bayern Munich, also chose to explore the same formula. Both teams alternated the likes of Pjanić, Busquets, Frenkie de Jong, Kimmich, Thiago Alcántara, Tolisso and Goretzka to form pairs to keep the midfielders such as Messi, Coutinho and Thomas Müller at bay.

Also in Germany, Lucien Favre's Borussia Dortmund put the recipe into practice by pairing Axel Witsel with Emre Can. Similarly, in Italy's Serie A, several of the most dominant teams have based the organisation of their midfield on the coexistence of two midfielders. This is the case of Stefano Pioli's Milan, combining Franck Kassié, Ismaël Bennacer and Sandro Tonali; of Gian Piero Gasperini's stimulating Atalanta, closing their midfield with the Freuler-De Room tandem behind Papu Gómez; or the significant example of Pirlo's Juventus, using Bentancur, Rabiot, McKennie or Arthur Melo to occupy with two players the space that, in his time as a player, the coach dominated alone.

As for the English Premier League, in addition to the aforementioned role of Ilkay Gündogan and Bernardo Silva at Guardiola's Manchester City, recent examples include Mourinho's Tottenham, Höjbjerg and Moussa Sissoko, and Solskjær's United, Fred and Scott McTominay.

Tell me how midfielders change, and I will tell you how football changes.

CHAPTER 7

"XAVI AND INIESTA CANNOT PLAY TOGETHER"

> "When you are a coach, you will want to put every midfielder in your team; it's the best way to play well"[210]
>
> PEP GUARDIOLA

Today it seems impossible, but there was a time when it was considered that Xavi and Iniesta could not play together. That despite the quality they were both recognised for, their simultaneous presence on the pitch unbalanced their team. It was understood that the sum between the two resulted in facets of the game that they could cover on their own, and that in exchange, aspects that neither of them were able to cover were stripped away. Before the two La Masía-trained midfielders formed a pairing that was so perfect that it was difficult to know where one ended and the other began, the idea was established that

---

210 Irigoyen, Juan I. (2013). Mascherano is always there. *Mascherano siempre está. El País.*

their coach would always have to choose between the two when it came to putting together the eleven.

Far from being a debate that remained in the realm of the fan or the media, the alleged incompatibility between Xavi and Iniesta was an issue that even penetrated the Barça dressing room. Its protagonists were no strangers to the discussion. They commented on it in 2006, interviewed in unison by Luis Martín for newspaper El País, shortly after losing to Internacional de Porto Alegre in the final of the Club World Cup[211]:

- Iniesta: I feel very bad about this situation. There came a day when I thought: but are we from different teams?

- Xavi: I really don't like it when people try to set us against each other. It happened to me with Guardiola and now it's happening to you and it's not fair.

- Iniesta: It's true. You spend all day listening, hearing things. It seems like they want me to get on badly with you and you have always helped me. (...) We can play together. I don't know where it's written that we can't do it. The problem is that they've been asking us to play together for I don't know how long, and they put us in Madrid, and we lose. Two days before was the best solution. It's not as if we were losing because we were playing together.

- Xavi: It's just that I have a great time with you. We are not clones, we are complementary.

Twelve years later, at the ceremony in which FC Barcelona bid farewell to Andrés Iniesta, who was ending his career as a player with the Catalan club, Xavi paid tribute to his former team-mate with a letter in which he also echoed the debate that at one point tried to distance them: "I, who have been a passer all my life, needed players like

---

211 Martín, Luís (2006). "We are children of the system". "*Somos hijos del sistema*". *El País.*

Andrés, like Lio, like Busi. You have been the best partners I've ever had. They always gave you the right outlet no matter how bad the situation was. I don't know where, but Andrés always came to me at the right time. Look at me, I'm here!'. But he didn't say it to me by talking. We didn't talk much on the pitch either, or we've played together for more than 10 years. We didn't need to. We understood each other by looking at each other (...). And to remember now that they said we couldn't play together..."[212].

As history would later show, Xavi and Iniesta could not only play together, but, as writer Sergi Pàmies pointed out, "they improved each other"[213]. They were already doing so, between 2005 and 2008, under Frank Rijkaard.

That the debate remained alive, even though the two youth players had already played together many times at Barça, is explained by the fact that, in reality, the sentence "Xavi and Iniesta cannot play together", incorporated, without needing to mention it, a third protagonist. A third actor without a specific name. What was defended between 2005 and 2008 when it was stated that Xavi and Iniesta could not play together was not so much that they could not share a line-up, but that, in order to do so, they had to play together with a different type of inside player. It was considered that Xavi and Iniesta could play together, but that they could not occupy at the same time the two places that the 1-4-3-3 reserves for the inside players. That alongside them, in front of the pivot, they needed the company of midfielders like Edgar Davids, Thiago Motta, Deco or Mark van Bommel. A dynamic and energetic pitbull, a future positional midfielder, a creative playmaker with a great feel for winning rejects, and a powerful finisher from the second line who, despite their obvious

---

212 Marca (2018). An emotional letter from Xavi to Iniesta: "And they said we couldn't play together..." *Emotiva carta de Xavi a Iniesta: "Y decían que no podíamos jugar juntos...". Marca.*

213 Pàmies, Sergi (2007). Iniesta and Xavi (and viceversa). *Iniesta y Xavi (y viceversa). La Vanguardia.*

differences, had one trait in common: their ability to add length and to defend without the ball.

Frank Rijkaard's team, like all football in general in those years, was organised in this way. From the sum of different players. Often forming pairs of opposing characteristics, so that what one didn't have, the other had. It was the era of double pivots, of combining an attacking full-back with another who acted practically as a third centre-back, of clearly differentiated profiles in the centre of the defence and of creative midfielders accompanied by a teammate. The era of David Albelda and Rubén Baraja, of Paolo Maldini and Cafú, of Ricardo Carvalho and John Terry, or of Andrea Pirlo and Gennaro Gattuso. The teams were not designed to point all the pieces in the same direction, but to configure a sort of showcase of virtues that covered all directions. Teams which, as coach Óscar Cano described in "El Modelo de juego del FC Barcelona", functioned as "a collection of closed properties"[214].

In that football, Xavi and Iniesta could play together, but only if one of them was in a position other than inside. As on one of the many occasions when, in Rijkaard's Barça, in the absence of Ludovic Giuly or Ronaldinho Gaucho, Andrés Iniesta took up a striker's position. Or when Xavi Hernández returned to being the midfielder who landed in the first team called upon to take over from Pep Guardiola. They could even do so when the coach opted to organise the team in a 1-3-4-3 formation, as the scheme allowed that in midfield, in addition to the pivot and the two youth players, there was room for that different inside player who was then understood to complete them. That Xavi and Iniesta could not play together was a lie, but a lie that, like so many in the history of football, at a particular time and in a particular place was true.

---

214 Cano, Oscar (2009), The FC Barcelona game model. A network of meaning interpreted from the paradigm of complexity. *El modelo de juego del FC Barcelona. Una red de significado interpretada desde el paradigma de la complejidad.* España: MCSports.

Thus, during the four years that separate the 2004-05 season and the 2007-08 season, Xavi and Iniesta played together as starters, and both occupying the two inside positions, a total of 37 matches of which Frank Rijkaard's Barça won less than half (18). A lower winning percentage than the one registered by the Blaugrana in those years, and also lower than the one achieved when Xavi and Iniesta were in the team but in different positions. For Xavi and Iniesta to be able to play together without the need for an intermediary, football had to change.

And it did. At the hands of Pep Guardiola who, even before taking on the adventure of the dugout and decisively crossing the path of his two most gifted pupils, had already given some clues as to how he understood the particularities of their game. For example, in March 2007, when, in a difficult period and on the verge of elimination from the Champions League at the hands of Liverpool, Rijkaard's Barça rescued a 1-3-4-3 formation from the memory chest, allowing the Dutch coach to play Xavi, Iniesta, Deco and Rafa Márquez in midfield behind three strikers and in front of three defenders. If the small three play," wrote Guardiola at the time in the pages of El País newspaper, "the home-grown players should be in charge of controlling and developing the game, and Deco should be in charge of finishing"[215].

Although at the time it was the Portuguese international who, of the three, made the greatest defensive contribution to the team, Pep imagined him closer to the opposition penalty area than to the engine room. Deco, a midfielder with a competitive gesture and Brazilian blood, accepted the risk of losing the ball as a necessary toll to accompany his inventiveness and creativity in three quarters of the pitch[216]. For Guardiola, however, a team's balance lay

215 Guardiola, Josep (2007). Feel it.*Sentirlo*. *El País newspaper.*

216 Roca, Marc (2013). *Ecos del balón*: Portuguese-Brazilian. *Luso-brasileño.* Extracted from: **http://www.ecosdelbalon.com/2013/09/retirada-deco-carrera-por-to-barcelona-rijkaard/**

in its ability not to lose the ball, and both Xavi and Iniesta did not. "Cruyff believes that what balances the game is the ball. Lose too many, and you are an unbalanced team. Lose too few, and it's all about balance"[217].

Having each other, in fact, made it even more difficult for one of the two youngsters to compromise their control of the ball. It was a virtue inherent to their game and their school, enhanced by the proximity of the right teammate. Not in vain, as Ricard Torquemada wrote in "Fórmula Barça. Journey to the interior of a team that has discovered eternity", one of the first instructions that Xavi Hernández received in the formative football of the Blaugrana team was that he could not lose the ball[218].

On this topic, the meeting between the coach from Santpedor and Patricia González, then coach of the Azerbaijan U-19 women's team, which Martí Perarnau recounts in "Herr Pep", is particularly illustrative. At one point in their chat, the coach asked Guardiola about how to identify good footballers, and Pep's answer could not have been clearer: "The really good ones are those who never lose the ball. The ones who pass the ball and don't lose it. Those are the good ones. And they are the ones who have to play, even if they have less of a name than others"[219].

The foundations of the postulate were laid by Johan Cruyff with one of his most celebrated explanations: "If you have the ball, the other team doesn't", under the umbrella of which he hid a large part of his playing philosophy. For the Dutch coach, being the team capable of having control of the ball meant taking the initiative in the

---

217 Guardiola, Josep (2006). Going out as a couple. *Salir de novios. El País*.

218 Torquemada, Ricard (2011). *Fórmula Barça. A journey inside the team that discovered eternity. Viatge a l'interior d'un equip que ha descobert l'eternitat.* Valls, España: Cossetània Edicions.

219 Perarnau, Martí (2014). Herr Pep. Feature behind his first year at Bayern Munich. *Herr Pep. Crónica desde dentro de su primer año en el Bayern Múnich.* Barcelona, España: Editorial Córner.

game, in order to determine the script of the match from that leading position. He decided on what terms the game would be played, and could therefore steer the match in the direction he wanted to take. Under this premise, the coexistence of Xavi and Iniesta in midfield not only did not subtract but multiplied the effects that each of them could have separately. If the player from Terrassa did not stand out for his exuberant deployment without the ball or for his ability to cover long distances at great speed, he did not need a partner to take on these tasks, but rather an ally to draw up a game in which it was not necessary to attend to them. If problems could arise when they didn't have the ball, it was a question of increasing the arguments for having it and for doing so in the most profitable way. To place Iniesta next to Xavi, not so that Andrés could run what the Catalan could not run, but so that neither of them had to do so.

In this sense, Pep Guardiola's intervention at Barcelona was not limited to putting Xavi and Iniesta together in the midfield but intensified the idea by accompanying them with a midfielder such as Sergio Busquets or populating the pitch with players with midfield intentions. To Javier Mascherano, who under his tutelage settled into the same central midfield role that had previously been occupied by another midfielder such as Yaya Touré, Pep once assured him that when he became coach, he would want to "put all the midfielders in your team; it's the best way for the team to play well". In addition to the repositioning of former pivots in the centre of defence, the Santpedor native's career in the dugouts has seen midfielders like Kimmich, Delph and Zinchenko playing as wingers, others like Iniesta, Thiago, David Silva, De Bruyne and Bernardo Silva occupying winger positions, or midfielders like Lio Messi, Mario Götze and Phil Foden placed in the centre-forward's home to link up with the midfield line as false nines.

Probably the episode that best symbolises the Catalan coach's preference for providing his teams with as many midfielders as possible is the final of the Club World Cup that Barça played against Santos with Muricy Ramalho, Ganso and Neymar Jr. That day, in Yokohama, the Blaugrana won with resounding authority by 4 goals to nil, presenting a starting eleven that, on paper, did not include any natural strikers. Alongside Víctor Valdés, Barça had Puyol, Piqué, Abidal, a Dani Alves who played not as a full-back but as a midfielder, and up to six players easily identifiable as holding midfielders, interior or inside wide midfielders or attacking playmaking midfielders: Sergio Busquets, Xavi Hernández, Andrés Iniesta, Cesc Fàbregas, Lio Messi and Thiago Alcántara. For a few minutes there were seven, when in the second half Javier Mascherano came on in place of Piqué. A 1-3-4-3 that, due to the lack of strikers, history has renamed 1-3-7-0[220]. A team without strikers.

Neymar, the Santos star, surrendered after the game to the display of those who would later become his teammates: "Today Barça taught us how to play football"[221]. Nor was coach Muricy Ramalho oblivious to his rival's performance, nor to the novel team without strikers that Guardiola had put in place: "Barcelona showed that it is possible to play well and score goals without any strikers"[222].

In addition to the number of midfielders that Barça lined up together against Santos, another of the peculiarities of Guardiola's approach that night was the affinity between the profiles of many of them. Where years before Xavi and Iniesta could not play together, now both shared the team's handle surrounded by players like Busquets, Cesc and Thiago Alcántara, all of them more or less direct heirs

220 Mundo D (2011). The 3-7-0, the new revolution of Guardiola's Barcelona. *El 3-7-0, la nueva revolución del Barcelona de Guardiola. Mundo D.*

221 Giner, Jorge (2017). Panenka: The 3-7-0 revolution. *Panenka: La revolución del 3-7-0.*Extracted from: https://www.panenka.org/miradas/la-revolucion-del-3-7-0/

222 Domènech, Joan (2011). Ramalho and the 3-7-0. *Ramalho y el 3-7-0. El Periódico de Catalunya newspaper.*

to the 4 that since Cruyff has distinguished the organisers of the Barça game. Members of the same lineage, of which their coach was also an emblem, which gives name and form to players who, despite their differences, are aligned with the same objective: to dominate the midfield through ball possession.

A purpose that has also been pursued in his teams by Spain international Sergio Canales, whether playing as a false winger like Thiago against Santos, as a playmaker like Cesc, as a deep-lying midfielder like Xavi and Iniesta or as a midfielder like Sergio Busquets. On the impact on his game of playing alongside team-mates with similar characteristics, the Betis midfielder said: "I like to be in a team that has the ball, that is in control of the game from possession, and for that you need players who want the ball and who are creative. If you have more players like that, you have more outlets and you won't have to carry that responsibility on your own. It's also true that attacking midfielders want to play a lot and touch the ball a lot, and that sometimes means that your participation drops or that you can end up stepping on their toes"[223].

Often, this quest to dominate the midfield in order to control the course of matches has been articulated around the figure of a highly participative midfielder who plays the role of orchestra conductor. A midfielder through whom all the team's moves pass, and whose boots he checks the ball as often as necessary to find the best route to the goal. A beacon. A guide. The brains of the team. The coach's extension on the pitch and a player with the freedom to move around the wide area, so that the ball always has the chance to reach his feet.

A figure that in Guardiola's Barça was embodied by Xavi Hernández, a player who became the symbol of an idea that Ricard Torquemada described in 2008 in the follow-

223 *En un momento dado* (2021). Interview with Sergio Canales. Extracted from: https://eumd.es/2021/04/entrevista-sergio-canales/

ing terms: "Naturally, Xavi is the glue that binds all the pieces together. When he has the ball, Barça comes together around him. Teams whose raison d'être is based on possession are organised through the ball, a responsibility that he has assumed since he started playing this sport (...), his presence corrects everything: he lubricates the circulation, applies the pause, acts as glue to bring the team together, decides the rhythm and activates the centre forwards"[224].

Hand in hand with his team's triumphs, the Catalan's play, characteristics, and gestures influenced an entire generation of midfielders, who moulded their footballing personalities in the heat of his influence. "Xavi influenced all Spanish players. He was a real star who changed the history of our country"[225], admits Ander Herrera, sharing the same opinion as Canales: "He is always been a reference point. It's been good for me to have seen Xavi play for so long (...). He is a player who has marked an era in midfield. Playing with one or two touches and controlling the tempo of the game, he was the best".

Sergio Canales' trajectory narrates a journey, usual in players of his characteristics, from the midfield to the centre circle. A path that started close to the front of the opposing box or was inclined towards one of the two flanks, which over the years led him to areas of the pitch that favoured a more continuous relationship with the ball. Areas that Xavi was familiar with from his time as a midfielder, and to which he also remained linked from the inside position. When I played more on the wing, as a winger, Hazard was one of my references," recalls Sergio, "because of his play on the wing and his ability to generate goals and chances from the flank, but with the change of position

---

224 Torquemada, Ricard (2008). Glued until 2014. *Pegamento hasta 2014. Mundo Deportivo.*

225 *En un momento dado* (2021). Interview with Ander Herrera. Extracted from: https://eumd.es/2021/04/entrevista-ander-herrera/

I began to look at other players such as Xavi, Modrić or Kroos".

The German, who underwent a similar conversion to that of Canales when he was no longer the playmaker that Jupp Heynckes lined up behind Mario Mandžukić and was transformed into the inside player to whom Guardiola handed the keys to his first Bayern, is considered by many to be the best heir to Xavi Hernández. Xavi himself invested him thus in 2017: "He is the engine of Real Madrid. He has a way of playing that reminds me a lot of me, he's like my successor on the pitch"[226]. A parallel that the Madrid player did not shy away from either when he stated that "many players of my generation who learned in that position were guided by Xavi and his game"[227].

With regard to Xavi Hernández's impact on the football of so many other midfielders with a taste for directing the play of their teams, the list of references is extensive. Koke Resurrección, for example, has pointed to him since his early days in the top flight as a reference point[228], Just like Ilkay Gündoğan, who in 2017 said of him: "I adored Xavi, he was always my role model and I looked up to him"[229]. Inter Milan midfielder Stefano Sensi, for his part, not only points to the Catalan as his idol, but also claims to have studied videos to imitate his movements on the pitch: "When I am compared to him, I get emotional"[230]. Arthur Melo, who arrived at the Camp Nou called to succeed Xavi

226 Marca (2017). Xavi: "Kroos is my successor on the pitch". *"Kroos es mi sucesor en el campo"*. *Marca newspaper*.

227 *Mundo Deportivo* (2017). Kroos: "Xavi is an example in many ways and also as a person. *"Xavi es un ejemplo en muchos aspectos también en lo personal"*. *Mundo Deportivo*.

228 Hidalgo, Dani (2012). "Xavi is my benchmark, but my idol was Juninho". *"Xavi es mi referente, pero mi ídolo era Juninho"*. *As*.

229 Castro, Juan (2017). Ilkay Gündogan: "My model has always been Xavi". *"Mi modelo siempre ha sido Xavi"*. *Marca*.

230 Prat, Irati (2020). *Soy Calcio*: Sensi: "Xavi is my idol, when I am compared to him I get emotional". *"Xavi es mi ídolo, cuando me comparan con él me emociono"*. Extracted from: http://soycalcio.com/2020/04/03/sensi-xavi-es-mi-idolo-cuando-me-comparan-con-el-me-emociono/

as the organiser of the Catalan side's play, also claimed to have the Terrassa native as a reference and mirror: "It's a style of play that I've been following since I was a child, always with the ball at my feet"[231].

One of the particularities acquired by this type of inside player is the relevance when his teams build the game from the back. When they are looking for a clean start that allows them to advance metres with the ball under control and keeping the block grouped around the ball. His involvement in these tasks takes a variety of forms, sometimes breaking into the midfield to receive the ball directly from the centre-backs, sometimes dropping to the wing in search of more space.

Sometimes dropping to the left like Kroos, Verratti, Gündoğan, Arthur Melo or De Jong, and sometimes moving to the right like Thiago, Kimmich, Modrić or Sergio Canales, it is a mechanism that aims to create a scenario in which these players are comfortable receiving the ball. To provide them with the best conditions to guide the team forward, as Eder Sarabia, who worked as assistant coach to Quique Setién at Las Palmas, Betis, and FC Barcelona, explains: "Sometimes we tried to put the midfielders in a position between centre-back and full-back, especially when we played with four at the back, because they are players who, in theory, have more quality and can get the ball out more easily"[232].

One of the men who was the protagonist of the manoeuvre, Sergio Canales, recalls how "I had never worked so hard on the ball as I did with Quique Setién. It was extraordinary how he gave a lot of solutions to all the players in each position. For the midfielders, we worked on the

---

231 Cadena Cope (2018). Arthur: "Xavi and Iniesta are my mirror but the comparison will not affect me". *"Xavi e Iniesta son mi espejo, pero la comparación no va a afectarme". Cadena Cope.*

232 Morén, Albert (2019). *En un momento dado:* "About full-backs and inside attacking midfielders". *Sobre laterales e interiores.* Extracted from: **https://eumd. es/2019/08/analisis-relacion-laterales-interiores/**

solution of having an inside player or, if we played with a double pivot, one of the centre midfielders, to play on the side of the central midfielder (...). It's very difficult for the opposing midfielder or the inside midfielder to follow you so far away when you lateralise the position. That's why you usually go to receive alone. And so the full-back or the wing-back stretches out wide and the winger can get inside. We had a solution in depth, another one between the lines, the option to change direction... We were always looking for three or four very clear options so that it was easier for the player. During the first part of the season it was something that hurt the opponents a lot. Then they got to know us, and it was a bit more difficult for us".

Precisely because of the importance that building play from the back has acquired in the teams' approach, as well as the impact that certain midfielders have in this phase of the game, the efforts of opponents have also increased when it comes to responding to it. More intense, advanced, and prepared pressures so that playing the ball close to the goalkeeper no longer means enjoying space and calmness that in other areas of the pitch were much more restricted. Pressure as a response and as a stimulus for a new ecosystem in midfield that marks the evolution of its protagonists. A context where receiving the ball with space and looking towards the opposing goal is less common than before.

It is a situation that demands new tools from the midfielders when it comes to inhabiting the same places, both individually and collectively. With regard to the former, the ability to protect the ball by receiving it with your back to goal and with an opponent close to you looking for a steal has gained in value, and has meant that those players who are used to playing without space near the opponent's area have also gained in importance playing in behind. Men accustomed to playing in particularly crowded areas, between the centre-backs and the opposition midfield, who have transferred their learning in the midfield to a

more backward area. "In my case, having played up front is something that helps me now that I play a bit further back," says Sergio Canales. "Especially when it comes to wanting the ball and not hiding to give the centre-backs a way out. I'm also good at coming forward from the second line. Having played further up the pitch helps me to be able to turn when I receive from the back in midfield, and also when I'm driving forward".

Regarding the play of the inside players, the response to the increased pressure from the opposition has been two-fold, often simultaneous. The first has consisted of keeping certain inside players close to the pivot's area. This behaviour is related to influencing the start of the action which, in this case, also serves as an aid for the team-mate under pressure. In the event that the latter's control of the ball is compromised, and the opponent's pressure does not allow him to move the ball forward with a pass, the close appearance of the inside player creates a bridge that is easy to cross so long as the ball finds an escape route[233].

A close ally, redundant in terms of the staggering of the midfield line, who sacrifices a more suitable positioning for the advance in exchange for ensuring the ball is kept. Interiors that at times take on the appearance of a second midfield, incorporating a piece at the back when the opposition's pressure is most stifling, with the aim of gaining an outlet. Kroos and Modrić when they occupied the interiors of Zinedine Zidane's Madrid, Ivan Rakitić when he was under Ernesto Valverde at Barcelona or certain stretches of Gündoğan at Guardiola's City all add their own names to the trend. "What Guardiola has been doing at certain times in recent years is to drop an inside player, who is normally

---

233 Cervera, Adrián (2020). The approach game. *El juego de aproximación*. España.

Gündoğan, close to the midfield," analyses Martí Perarnau on this issue[234].

However, the resource of delaying the position of one of the inside midfielders by moving him closer to the midfield, coexists with a second trend: the development of deep midfielders, more unbalanced and linked to the attacking midfield. Following the thread of Manchester City, since Pep Guardiola has been in charge of their midfield, the likes of David Silva, Kevin de Bruyne, Bernardo Silva and Phil Foden have passed through their midfield, and Gündogan himself has displayed an unexpectedly powerful version, projecting himself into attack and bursting into the box in search of a finish. Midfielders who either naturally or induced, move away from the midfield and towards the centre-forward.

Using inside players in this way, first of all, allows their teams to make more direct use of the spaces that the opponent allows behind the pressure, so that if the goalkeeper, the defenders, or the pivot manages to filter the pass behind the midfield, the inside player can attack with space in front of him and with few opposing players between him and the goal. It is a measure that places the responsibility for the outlet on the boots of the players further back, in exchange for providing them with a greater number of forward passing options.

"Nowadays the midfielder has to cover a lot of space. If you can dominate both areas you have a lot to gain," says Canales. "Breaking lines with a drive is gold. With the high pressing and how well positioned the teams are, players like De Jong or Modrić, who overcome lines with a dribble and give the pass to the last line, break schemes".

The other scenario in which this way of using the inside players has the most impact is when facing a defensive system situated close to their own goal. When the team

---

234 *En un momento dado* (2021). Interview with Martí Perarnau. Extracted from: https://eumd.es/2021/04/entrevista-marti-perarnau/

manages to break the opposition's pressure and is pushed back by a large number of players in the vicinity of the box. Those in which the attack is reduced in space and in which the opponent is in a better position to close cracks through which they can be wounded. In this respect, Pep Guardiola acknowledged to Perarnau that his time on the bench away from Messi had forced him to improve as a coach because, without Lio, the coach was faced with the need to provide his players with solutions that the Argentinian, at Barça, was able to find more independently. His slate had to cover a part of the game that, before, he could delegate to Messi's talent.

In a way, separating himself from Lio made him break one of the premises of his time as Barça coach, according to which his job was to get the team up top in the best possible conditions, so that there, in the final metres, the responsibility would return to the players' boots. Without Messi, the coach's hand had to go further.

The advanced presence of the inside players, therefore, is one of the mechanisms that the Catalan coach has rescued to respond to this new need. As a way to hit opposing defensive systems, opening them up through the vision of his midfielders, their ability to burst into the box or their ability to progress with the ball until they get an opposing player out of position. "In basketball you attack the basket and when the opponent closes down you take the ball out and shoot the three-pointer. In football it's the same: you have to attack the forwards; you have to attack the centre-backs and you have to attack the centre-backs (...). The centre-back or the midfielder has to attack the opposing pivots. He has to make them come out, because otherwise they stay there and the space behind them doesn't exist. And then those who receive the ball at the back have to attack the centre-backs. That's where the chances come from", explained Pep in an interview with Gol Televisión[235].

In it, Guardiola also referred to how, in attack, there are certain areas that are indefensible. Areas of the pitch which, when they are conquered, either the opponent has no antidote or the application of such an antidote involves other equally lethal concessions. Although in the interview the coach from Santpedor kept it a secret, it is generally agreed that one of the indefensible areas he referred to is precisely one that is very directly linked to the advanced use of the inside players: the space between the full-back and the opposing team's centre-back.

These two lanes are enlarged as the width of the wingers pulls the full-backs towards the flanks, and the mobility of the striker attracts the attention of the centre-backs on the inside. Two open corridors, perfect for the vertical irruption of interior players who are authorised to become strikers, as a nod to the systems of the past that populated the attack with the presence of up to five players[236].

Cracks in the defence through which to access the inside of the box, conquer the back line, turn the opposing defence and make them run backwards. A dagger between the ribs with which to break the opposition's order, shake up their measured defensive positioning and provoke the appearance of new spaces to get closer to the goal.

This advanced use of inside players, with an exaggerated attacking vocation and proximity to the strikers, Pep knew first-hand as captain of Louis van Gaal's Barça. That was a period of footballing maturity for Guardiola, marked by his admiration for the work that the Dutchman had previously carried out at Ajax, as he himself mentioned in

---

235 GOL (24th July, 2019). 90 minutes with Pep Guardiola. Extracted from: https://youtu.be/hNCjnwKEea4

236 Manna, Matías (2014)."Paradigma Guardiola: 2-3-5. a return to first tactics". *Paradigma Guardiola: 2-3-5, el retorno a la primera táctica*. Extracted from: http://paradigmaguardiola.blogspot.com/2014/04/2-3-5-el-retorno-de-la-primera-tactica.html

the book "La meva gent, el meu futbol": "Few teams, and I have seen many play, have seduced me with the intensity with which that one did. Few, very few, but for many reasons. For the great individual talent they showed. For the exhibition of collective play. For the ease with which they started to build from the back. For the speed of their wingers and the way they passed the ball. To the foot, to the space. And I was also seduced by the sense and astuteness with which Kluivert and Kanu, the strikers, opened up space to create the space for the second line to finish. They were fantastic because, in addition, that Ajax team had the ability to solve all the one-on-ones that could be found in a match in an excellent way. The same in defence as in attack: they took all the risks that a team is capable of taking"[237].

At the age of 26, the player had developed a voracious curiosity for the secrets and whys and wherefores of football, and his appetite found the best possible nourishment in endless football talks with his new coach.

Louis van Gaal had landed in Barcelona backed by the successes of a Cartesian Ajax, in which each player's place obeyed the needs of the collective plan: "The thing is that Ajax always gave me the feeling that they wanted to do this. To play, to sacrifice as a collective, to shine individually and to win games. All their players, of different quality, but all of them, without exception, were aware of their mission on the pitch. The discipline of positions. Possession of the ball as a basic idea. Playing with constant help. Two-touch movement... And they did it all in a way that was as simple as it was sublime. There are other ways of achieving it, but I liked and still like the way Van Gaal's Ajax gave football lessons to everyone"[238].

---

237 Guardiola, Josep (2001). My people, my football. *La meva gent, el meu futbol.* Barcelona, España: EDECASA, Grupo Z.

238 Guardiola, Josep (2001). My people, my football. *La meva gent, el meu futbol.* Barcelona, España: EDECASA, Grupo Z.

The experience at the Camp Nou, however, required Van Gaal to adapt to a different set of players to those he had had in Amsterdam, especially his star player: Rivaldo. The Brazilian, brought in to take Ronaldo Nazario's place as the team's new standard-bearer, arrived in Barcelona with the task of spearheading the project from the pitch, but without a clear place from which to do so. A creative left-footed playmaker with a taste for unrestricted movement in attack, his desire for freedom did not sit too well with Van Gaal's strict slate.

In the end, the position the coach found for him was that of left winger, an area from which, for years, the player and the coach fought a battle between the autonomy demanded by the former and the straightness demanded by the latter. To achieve a balance between the two, the team played a counterbalancing game thanks to its inside players, positions most commonly occupied by Luis Enrique and Phillip Cocu. These two players assumed a starting position at Guardiola's side, the midfield, but as the attacking play progressed, they were released from the midfield to move to the flanks or into the box.

For Guardiola that situation had two sides to it. With the ball, the advanced position of his midfield partners multiplied the passing options across the width of the pitch. Without the ball, on the other hand, it often created a loneliness in the centre circle that was far removed from the shelter that Cruyff had provided years earlier, which the architect of the "Dream Team" explained as follows: "With Guardiola, what we always did was that wherever he played he was packed in, that he never had to defend too much space. Always a reduced space. So it's just a question of seeing, nothing more. I always had to keep an eye on one thing: to have two team-mates close to me so that I only had to defend a small space. That way you're the best defender there is"[239].

---

239 *Recorda Míster* (2009). "Johan Cruyff". Barça TV

As a coach, the decision to have the full-backs join the attack on the inside to populate the vicinity of the pivot, even when the two inside backs are separated from him, has helped him to remedy the abandonment: "The key is in the two full-backs, who when they have the ball in front of them close in next to the midfielder and form a line of three that protects us from counter-attacks. With this life-line, it is possible to play five forwards because you have the back four covered"[240].

Those seasons with Van Gaal at Barcelona also seemed to leave their mark on Luis Enrique. The Asturian, the perfect image of versatility in his time as a player, was one of the men most commonly used by the coach in the inside position, although his goalscoring figures could well have made him one of the team's strikers. In part he was, as two of his main roles related to the centre-forward and winger areas. In the former, he would burst in from the second line to occupy the shooting area when the mobile Patrick Kluivert moved away from the box. In the second, he would alternate with Luis Figo so that the Portuguese could come inside.

Years later, as Barça coach and managing Leo Messi, Luis Enrique applied similar concepts to the position he most often occupied as a Barça player, as Denis Suárez explained to Miguel Quintana in an interview in 2021: "With Luis Enrique the inside right was a bit different, because you had to combine positions with Messi. If Lio came inside, you had to go to the wing. Luis Enrique considered that I had the route to make that movement from the inside to the outside"[241].

It is an inside movement that has also been used by other teams looking to benefit wingers with inside weight.

---

240 Perarnau, Martí (2016). Pep Guardiola. The metamorphosis. *Pep Guardiola. La metamorfosis.* Barcelona, España: Editorial Córner.

241 Quintana, Miguel (29th March, 2021). The story of Denis Suárez: a talent without a fixed position. Extracted from:https://**youtu.be/-Q8sEB18U38**

Whether it is to make it easier for them to land on the edge of the box or inside the area, wing forwards such as Cristiano Ronaldo, Neymar, Bale, Sterling, Mane or Mohamed Salah have found their perfect allies in the figure of wingers capable of getting close to the touchline such as Angel Di María, De Bruyne, James Milner, Wijnaldum, Jordan Henderson and Luka Modrić, of whom Juande Ramos, his coach when he joined Tottenham in the Premier League, says that "he has the ability to do any job from midfield forward. In that area he can do any role. He is a very intelligent player in attacking tasks and in directing play"[242].

The positional evolution of inside players, and their increasingly close association with attacking positions, has also led to a change in the most distinctive traits of the players who embody this role. For a start, as their relationship with the strikers has become closer, their ability to assist and provide the final pass has increased in value. Their impact on games is no longer just near the centre circle and in terms of directing play but goes directly into their ability to create goalscoring chances. In a football that relies much less than in the past on the classic figure of the 10, players such as David Silva, Isco Alarcón, Christian Eriksen, Bernardo Silva, Emil Forsberg, James Maddison, Donny van de Beek, Bruno Fernandes, Giovani Lo Celso, Martin Odegaard or Stefano Sensi have transferred part of the emblematic essence of the playmaker to the inside positions.

Apart from their profile and, in many cases, the fact that they have moved from the playmaker, one of the issues that has resulted from this is the proliferation of inside players playing on the left. Right-footed players are lined up on the left side of midfield, and left-footed players on the right, with the aim of promoting more vertical profiles. "In this way, they are better profiled for the shot and the

---

242 *En un momento dado* (2021). Interview with Juande Ramos. Extracted from: https://eumd.es/2021/04/entrevista-juande-ramos/

final pass," commented Jaume Mercet, a journalist specialising in Barça's youth teams, on the subject of players like Carles Aleñá and Álex Collado.

In the same vein, Sara Monforte, coach of Villarreal CF Femenino, said in 2018 about the then Barça player Nataša Andonova: "Playing with her left foot favours her to define from the second line with her left foot. She is more vertical. The more attacking a midfielder is, the more it benefits him to play with his left foot," adds Àlex Delmàs, "because at any moment he can go towards the box, to shoot or to look for the wall that will guide him to the finish. I was a midfielder with a finishing touch, with a shot, and that's why it was better for me to play on the opposite foot to take the diagonal into the box".

Delmàs' final comment, referring to the type of inside player who can most benefit from a position on the opposite foot, ties in with the observation of former player and analyst Alberto Edjogo, when he points out that "for an attacking inside player, who can drive and hit, playing on the opposite foot can be fantastic. He can shoot, he can face up to the ball or he can receive a second ball that falls from the striker, oriented towards goal. However, a more organisational inside player will probably find it more difficult to face outwards. He will often have to play with his back to goal and waste time getting his shape right"[243].

Another fundamental trait in the evolution of the functions of the inside players has to do with overflow. With the ability to dribble, not from the flank like the classic wingers, but from the central lane, tearing through the opponent's defensive systems. It is not for nothing that the list of inside forwards who, before becoming wing forwards, added new names year after year.

Probably one of the most paradigmatic episodes on this issue is that of Bayern Munich itself, which Guardiola

243 Morén, Albert (2018). Two inside attacking midfielders playing on opposite ends. Extracted from: https://eumd.es/2018/09/interiores-a-pierna-cambiada/

coached for three seasons. The German squad, with players such as Arjen Robben, Franck Ribéry, Xherdan Shaqiri, Douglas Costa and Kingsley Coman, offered the coach from Santpedor a different type of striker to those he had had at Barcelona. A striker profile more in line with the traditional role of the classic winger, with a lot of outside edge and the ability to gain metres in front of goal thanks to his imbalance. As well as using them on the wing, however, Pep also used them at times in more central areas, using the impact of their dribbling to take on opposing pivots and centre-backs.

"Under Guardiola I have progressed. Tactically I've become more intelligent thanks to him. I don't just play as a right winger anymore, sometimes I play inside, sometimes in the centre. Pep has made me more variable," explained Robben about these changes of position[244].

Ribéry to face Hertha Berlin in 2014, Arjen Robben to Hamburg in 2015 or Douglas Costa to Hoffenheim or Atlético de Madrid in 2016, as representatives of the inner imbalance that Guardiola previously found in Andrés Iniesta and later in players like Bernardo Silva, Phil Foden or Kevin de Bruyne, and that others have sought in players like Di María, Roque Mesa, Michael Krohn-Dehli, Julian Brandt, Giovanni Reyna, Riqui Puig, Kai Havertz or Mason Mount.

Interiors with which to transfer to the central lane virtues that had usually corresponded to the wingers. When not, directly, wing forwards taken from their original position to play on the inside. "Look at me, the standard-bearer of midfielders, playing with five forwards!"[245].

---

244 Sport (2015). Robben: "The football by Pep Guardiola is a pleasure". *"El fútbol de Pep Guardiola es un placer". Sport.*

245 Perarnau, Martí (2016). *Pep Guardiola. La metamorfosis.* Barcelona, España: Editorial Córner.

CHAPTER 8

PLAYING WITH A MIDFIELDER AND TWO INVERTED WINGERS

> "Teams do not begin from back to front. For me they start with a midfielder and two inverted wingers"[246]
>
> PEP GUARDIOLA

Many of the terms used to describe football are shortcuts. They have to be, because they are often used to paint a fixed picture of a sport that is dynamic and changing. In football, things are not simply the way they are because they happen to be so, they happen and there are reasons behind them. Trying to capture them, therefore, is necessarily an approximate exercise, which, despite its usefulness, is aware of the sin it contains in itself. Its complexity does not fit into a still instant, even if this serves as a starting point.

---

246 Manna, Matías (2012). *Paradigma Guardiola*. Badalona, España: Ara Llibres.

This is the case with the numerical descriptions of the schemes used by the teams, as a tool for drawing their order on the pitch. The 1-4-4-4-2, the 1-3-4-3, the 1-5-3-2, the 1-4-2-3-1 and so many other formulas with which the eleven protagonists are distributed on paper, are in reality a more theoretical than practical order. They are almost an abstraction, as the dynamism of the game and the behaviour of the players are in permanent dispute. The only moment in which this pre-planned order of play is correctly implemented is just before the start of the match. The starting whistle is the end of it. A line-breaker!

The fragility of the terms when it comes to reflecting the reality of football has led not only to their questioning, but even to their outright rejection. An amendment to the whole. César Luis Menotti's famous and much-used reference to this is: "4-2-3-1, 3-4-5-1... that's a telephone number. Di Stéfano was once asked how it was possible for them to play a 2-3-5 and he replied: 'But what do you think that we used to be stupid, that with two guys we could defend five? We were all defending and those who knew how to attack were attacking"[247]. The Argentinian coach was thus responding to a certain trend, more typical of the field of journalism and criticism, which at certain times has reduced the footballing question, the nature of the teams and the outcome of the result to the drawings of the two contenders, ignoring their incomplete condition as a tackle. As if the terms were not a beginning from which to approach a more difficult, broader, and more nuanced reality, but an end with which to simplify a much more labyrinthine truth.

Despite their limitations, however, numerical descriptions of team schemes are not empty continents. They do not contain complete information, but they do offer a degree of insinuation. More as a hint than as a conclusion. The freedom of the 22 players on the pitch allows any initial order to

---

247 Martín, Luis (2011). "Football has been stolen from the people". *El fútbol se lo robaron a la gente*. El País.

be transformed into a multitude of different orders; in fact, it is common for the same team to change formation from one phase of the game to another, projecting the full-backs in attack, changing the staggering of their midfielders, centring the position of their theoretical wing forwards, or adding one of their attackers to the midfield when the team does not have the ball. As soon as the ball starts to roll on the pitch, what is expressed is not a pre-established scheme but one in permanent mutation. As Domènec Torrent, Guardiola's former assistant at Barcelona, Bayern Munich and Manchester City explained: "If I were a tactics teacher at a coaching school, I wouldn't fail anyone: no system counteracts another. It depends on the behaviour of the players"[248].

All patterns can lead to others, but as starting points, some encourage certain patterns and movements more than others. Thus, although it is not the norm, it is most common for a team that closes in at the back with a five-man defence to protect the centre of their area with three players; for a 1-4-4-2 to load the opposing centre-backs with a second threat at the back; or for a 1-4-2-3-1 to have two players on each of the flanks. All schemes allow for everything, but in some the path is more marked. As a result, certain coaches, teams or models of play tend to be more closely linked to one than the other. This is the case of FC Barcelona, whose relationship with the Dutch school has been linked to the 1-4-3-3 formula since the end of the 1990s when a fourth defender was added to Johan Cruyff's 1-3-4-3.

In this sense, as the journalist Adrián Blanco and Àlex Delmàs talked about in the podcast "Un Juego Perfecto", the 1-4-3-3 is a friendly system with an idea of play that is closely linked to dominance in the opposition half. It provides great width on the flank that takes advantage of the dimensions of the pitch to generate space, it facilitates

---

248 Torres, Diego (2020). Domènec Torrent: "If you lose the style, when you lose you have nothing left". *"Si pierdes el estilo, cuando pierdes no te queda nada". El País.*

the players being staggered at a multitude of heights, it encourages the positions of the players to create triangles so that the ball possessor always has passing options, and it groups the team around the ball in such a way that it allows for a more comfortable application of both combination play and pressure after a loss[249].

That is why it has been the most common formation in Pep Guardiola's teams, and why the contagion effect caused by his victories has given the formation renewed popularity in world football. This is how Ricardo La Volpe recognises it, when he argues that "Guardiola was very important in bringing the 1-4-3-3 back into use, after a few years in which the majority used 1-4-4-2 or 1-4-4-1-1"[250].

As of 2010, the list of representatives in the European competition is extensive. FC Barcelona, Real Madrid, Sevilla, Athletic Bilbao, Celta de Vigo, Real Sociedad, Manchester City, Liverpool, Chelsea, Manchester United, Arsenal, Leicester City, Bayern Munich, Borussia Dortmund, RB Leipzig, Juventus, Napoli, AS Roma, Paris Saint Germain, Olympique Lyonnais... all, at some point during the decade, have sought refuge in the 1-4-3-3 to achieve their objectives[251].

In the same way, in 2019 journalist Vicente Muglia reviewed in the sports daily Olé how 14 of the 24 teams in the first division of football in Argentina had used this same design: "In Argentine football, a trend began to emerge with Martino's Newell's in 2012/13 (...) is confirmed. It's an ideal system for triangulations. I copied it from Barcelona

249 *Ecos del balón* (5th March, 2020). A perfect game - the 4-3-3: A system to dominate. *Un juego perfecto - El 4-3-3: Un sistema para dominar.* Extracted from: https://www.ivoox.com/un-juego-perfecto-el-4-3-3-un-sistema-audios-mp3_rf_48518576_1.html

250 *En un momento dado* (2021). Interview with Ricardo La Volpe. Extracted from: https://eumd.es/2021/04/entrevista-ricardo-la-volpe/

251 Rodríguez, Francisco (2020). *Vip Deportivo*: The 4-3-3 is trend-setting. *El 4-3-3 marca tendencia.* Extracted from: https://vipdeportivo.es/el-4-3-3-marca-tendencia/

when I arrived at Newell's,' acknowledged Tata. In recent years there have been several exponents of this model: Jorge Almirón's Lanús, Guillermo Barros Schelotto's Boca, Ariel Holan's Defensa Y Justicia and Independiente, and Sebastián Beccacece's runners-up Defensa Y Justicia, among others"[252].

The popularity of the 1-4-3-3 has gone hand in hand with the esteem for one of its most representative figures: the winger. A wide player in a more advanced position than that reserved for him in any other scheme. He is as much a striker as the striker, but he is positioned close to the goal rather than inside the box.

The link between the 1-4-3-3 and the wingers is old, close, and motivated by several factors, one of the main ones being their ability to widen the field in attack. Playing on the wing and in a very advanced position, together with the full-backs, they complete a square that stretches the pitch towards the four corners of the pitch, forcing the opposition, when defending, to cover more space. Through the position of the wingers the attack is wide because it occupies the front from side to side, and it is also extensive because it does so from high up. It stretches towards the touchlines and towards the back line. Ricard Torquemada analysed the importance of the wingers in relation to their position in the following terms: "If the wingers are low, that is, shallow, the opposing centre-backs have the centre-forward as a reference and the opposition can bring the lines together more by taking a step forward to make the pitch smaller. On the other hand, if the wingers stretch the pitch, the centre-backs can no longer get out, because they neglect their backs, and any deep pass is a goal-scoring option"[253].

---

252 Muglia, Vicente (2019). The 4-3-3 is in command. *Manda el 4-3-3. Olé newspaper*.

253 Torquemada, Ricard (2011). *Fórmula Barça. A journey inside the team that discovered eternity. Viatge a l'interior d'un equip que ha descobert l'eternitat*. Valls, España: Cossetània Edicions.

Unlike other players who intervene on the edges of the pitch by getting into position, the winger waits in position, pinned as close to the corner flag as possible and setting beforehand as large a field of play boundary as the actual dimensions of the pitch will allow. As such, the winger has traditionally been a role closely associated with patience, as an important part of his usefulness has to do with his positioning rather than his ball handling. Part of his contribution is even made without touching the ball.

As an example of this, an anecdote revealed by Andoni Zubizarreta to Barça TV about Johan Cruyff's first pre-season as coach: the *Dream Team* goalkeeper recalled that after one of the many matches the team played in Papendal to assimilate the coach's new ideas for the start of the season, Txiki Begiristain was unhappy with his performance. He had barely made contact with the ball, and he understood that this meant that his game had not been good and that Cruyff would show him that the following morning. To his surprise, says Zubizarreta, the coach praised him as the best player of the game, making special emphasis on how his open position on the wing had been key to allowing the others to play more comfortably[254]. It didn't take long for the winger to understand this, and a few days later he would declare that "there are moments when I feel absent because I don't get the ball (...) but I understand that this is part of the system"[255].

By staying wide and close to the touchline, the winger not only widens the pitch, giving space to his teammates, but also forces the opposition defence to reach further out. The winger guarding him is forced to play further away from the cover of the centre-backs and midfielders.

---

254 *Recorda Míster* (2009). "Johan Cruyff". Barça TV.
255 Morén, Albert (2016). *En un momento dado: Aquel primer verano en Papendal.* "That first summer in Papendal". Extracted from: **https://eumd.es/2016/01/primer-verano-johan-cruyff-barcelona/**

Jeffrén Suárez trained as a winger in the youth ranks at FC Barcelona, where he completed the various stages that eventually led him to join the first team under Pep Guardiola. "When I was young, I was more of a playmaker. The free player who moved all over the place. When I arrived at Barça I first started playing as an inside player, but I had a coach who put me as a winger because of my speed and from then on, I stayed in that position," the Venezuelan recalls. A team-mate of Messi, Xavi, Iniesta and Sergio Busquets between 2009 and 2011, on the importance of the winger in a model of play like the *Culé*, Jeffren underlines how "the winger position helps the inside players a lot. If you want the inside player to receive a lot of balls between the lines, the centre-forward and the two wingers are the ones who are going to fix the opposition's defensive line. They are going to make the inside or inverted wingers receive a lot of balls, and at the end of the day they are the ones who create play"[256].

The marker of a winger finds it more difficult to get close to his teammates to reduce space for the opposing attack, and these, in turn, are further away from possible help on the wing. For this reason, because the winger's fixation makes it easier for the opposition to get close to him with only one player, the winger's job has also often been closely linked to dribbling. If he is patient waiting in the right place, his team will find it easier to serve him the ball, and when he receives it, he will be in a position to face a one-on-one situation against the defender. Set the position, receive the ball and face the opponent.

"Who are our unstoppable men? On the outside, Ribéry and Robben. So we have to go on the outside. Be superior on the inside, but open diagonally outwards. We have to bring the team up, bring it up a lot so that the two of them don't have to start the play so low", Guardiola said in Mu-

---

256 *En un momento dado* (2021). Interview with Jeffren Suárez. Extracted from: https://eumd.es/2021/04/entrevista-jeffren-suarez/

nich, as Martí Perarnau reports in the book *"Herr Pep"*[257]. A trend that, forced to solve attacking scenarios without an individuality of the calibre of Leo Messi, the coach has also followed in Manchester in the boots of players like Leroy Sané, Riyad Mahrez and Phil Foden. "I just ask: does this player dribble? I want players who dribble. That's the main question I ask. I want full-backs who dribble, and centre-backs and central and attacking midfielders and wingers who dribble. Because control and passing can be learnt... But I want them to dribble and go, that's key"[258].

It so happens that the popularity of the 1-4-3-3 that followed Pep Guardiola's successes, and the consequent revival of the use of inside wingers, coincided with a time when they were a rare commodity. At least, conceived as a dribbling and eminently wing-forward type. Football looked again to wingers when it was no longer producing them.

One of the factors often cited to explain the gradual disappearance of the classic winger is in the area of training. According to this theory, the rise and influence of proposals more oriented towards a type of play that especially penalises the loss of the ball, would have favoured the censoring of a risky gesture such as dribbling in favour of passing in the lower categories. To dribble is to expose oneself to a final verdict, to an action with no middle ground in which, if the player achieves his goal, he obtains an important advantage, but if he does not, he compromises possession. When you watch a youth football match and a kid dribbles, if he gets it right, they don't say anything, but if the dribble goes wrong the first expression you hear is: "but pass it!", reflected Manolo Márquez, a coach with experience in the leagues of Spain, Croatia, India and Thailand, in conversation with analyst and former player Alberto Edjogo. "The

---

257 Perarnau, Martí (2014). *Herr Pep. Crónica desde dentro de su primer año en el Bayern Múnich.* Barcelona, España: Editorial Córner.

258 Perarnau, Martí (2016). *Pep Guardiola. La metamorfosis.* Barcelona, Spain: Editorial Córner.

child has to learn to make mistakes, to lose the ball, to know when he has to pass and when he can dribble"[259].

Óscar García, who trained as a player at Barça's La Masía and whose career as a coach has taken him to teams such as Maccabi Tel Aviv, Brighton Hove and Albion, RB Salzburg, Saint-Étienne and Celta de Vigo, is along the same lines: "We have to change the base a little. We have to know which player has certain characteristics and which player has others in order to strengthen that. In grassroots football you have to prioritise the player. There are wide players who are very good at dribbling, but you can't ask them to just control and pass"[260].

When I started playing as a winger, I loved the one-on-one," recalls Jeffrén Suárez, "I loved feeling superior against the full-back and if I lost it I would try again. And if I lost the ball I would try again, why can't you lose the ball? I was always told to try, to take advantage of the fact that I had the necessary qualities to play as a winger. I had pace, dribbling, I could go out on the right or on the left.

In parallel to the training issue, a number of developments have taken place in top-level football that have altered the role of wingers in relation to their teams, opponents and their own place on the pitch. The disappearance of the playmaker is the common origin of several of them. The progressive abandonment of a particularly emblematic figure in the nineties, which served as a home for the most creative and free-scoring players in the team. A refuge from which they could play their football with fewer tactical ties than the rest, often freed from a large part of the defensive work and with the front of the box as a launch-

---

259 Edjogo-Owono, Alberto (24th February, 2020). How has modern football evolved? Aspects of the game with Manolo Márquez. *¿Cómo ha evolucionado el fútbol moderno? Los aspectos del juego con Manolo Márquez*. Extracted from: **https://youtu. be/kuZDjtdFMOk**

260 Diario As (4th March, 2020). Óscar García and the position of the winger in today's football. - "*Óscar García y la posición de extremo en el fútbol actual*" | *Futbología* #12. Extracted from: **https://youtu.be/L8o9gJ3QxrU**

ing pad. The place of the different. The one occupied by Maradona, Platini, Ronaldinho, Zidane, Riquelme, Rivaldo, Totti, Roberto Baggio or Juan Carlos Valerón. "That position no longer exists," lamented Zico in December 2018, "now in almost all teams they play with three or four in the middle, but in a linear fashion. And there is no room for a playmaker there"[261].

The popularity of schemes such as the 1-4-3-3 that renounce the playmaker to incorporate a third player in midfield, as well as the commitment to a more choral distribution of roles in which there is no room either for specialists in containment unattached to the ball or attacking artists without defensive involvement, changed the paradigm of midfield. At the same time, moreover, the increasing difficulty for the playmaker to find space between the lines in the era of double pivots, and the suspicion that his runs to get in contact with the ball in more positional proposals aroused, ended up shaping a hostile context for those players used to playing just behind the centre-forward.

"Playing behind the striker? What is it like? You don›t play behind the striker on the right? You don't play behind the striker on the left? You don't have to be in the centre?"[262]. This is how Johan Cruyff referred to the position in 2015, as sporting advisor to Chivas Guadalajara, when he was questioned about Marco Fabián's fit with the Mexican side [263]. The Dutchman understood the area traditionally identified with midfielders in a different way. As coach of Ajax Amsterdam and FC Barcelona, Cruyff had used a player in front of the midfield and just behind the centre-forward, but his characteristics and attributes had little to do with those of the classic 10.

---

261 Ruiz, Marco (2018). Zico: "The last great attacking midfielder was played by Zidane: it was Isco". *"El último gran mediapunta lo puso Zidane: era Isco". AS Newspaper.*

262 *Azteca América* (2012, junio 20). What is an attracking midfielder for Cruyff? Extracted from: https://youtu.be/k77KwCgD1Ug

263 Expósito, José María (2012). Cruyff signs as technical director with Chivas of Guadalajara. *El Periódico de Catalunya.*

In fact, in "El Flaco's" football this player was known as the 6, and such was his importance that on more than one occasion the coach had referred to it as the main novelty of his system. A sort of pivot playing with his back to the opposing goal who, positioned in front of the midfield, Cruyff used this so that the midfielders could always receive the ball facing him: "He wasn't the type of player who would get the ball, make a move... No, in this team we didn't want a player like that in that position"[264].

José Mari Bakero was the player who played this role the longest under Johan, a player who specialised in unloading the ball from the back with his first touch and who also incorporated virtues such as finishing and predisposition in pressing into his game. "What Bakero did very well was to play the ball with his first touch, and first touch is rhythm. And he always played the ball to people when it came in front of him. So, if you do that, you increase the pace. The axis between the 4 and the 6, together with the inside players and the forwards, he had an enormous ball speed and hardly lost any balls. And if you don't lose balls in the build-up, it's very difficult to be counter-attacked," Cruyff explained to FC Barcelona's official television station[265].

Over time, however, the need to reinforce the team with more or less a fixed presence of a fourth defender meant that the 1-3-4-3-3 gave way to the 1-4-3-3-3, and Cruyff's figure of the playmaker faded away. But its echoes remained. Several of his functions were not lost but were entrusted to a new type of centre-forward. One especially promoted from the Dutch school, who would combine his duties as an attacking reference with a rich back play, the ability to leave the area and an associative sensibility more typical of midfielders than the classic box-to-box finisher. For players such as Patrick Kluivert, Dennis Berg-

---

264 *Recorda Míster* (2009). "Johan Cruyff". Barça TV.
265 *Recorda Míster* (2009). "Johan Cruyff". Barça TV.

kamp or Nwankwo Kanu, the role of centre-forward would go beyond the final contact with the ball to put it into the goal and would actively participate in many of the moments prior to that. The striker would not only be the final destination, but also part of the journey.

The generalisation of the idea, after Pep Guardiola's successes on the bench in taking that same heritage and taking it to its most exaggerated version with the recovery of the figure of the false 9, has ended up presenting the wingers with a very different general context. With the 9 involved in the play outside the box, being less of a fixed reference for the finish and more of a mobile element in charge of building advantages away from his traditional natural habitat. Many teams have stopped asking their wingers to play a game adapted to the canon. They have stopped entrusting them to progress parallel to the flank, which today increasingly belongs to the full-backs, dribbling towards the corner and the measured cross to the penalty spot in search of a finisher whose presence is no longer assured. The hollowing out of the midfield changed the strikers, and these, in turn, gave birth to another type of winger, less linked to the goalmouth and more connected to the central lane.

This is how Miguel Ángel Portugal put it to newspaper Marca, analysing the reasons for the extinction of the classic wingers: "Times are changing. There is a demand for more inside passes and second line arrivals rather than crosses for headers. Maybe not only because of the lack of wingers, but also because of the loss of finishers like Santillana, Zamorano, Müller and company. Players like that exist very few and far between"[266].

Juande Ramos, a coach who throughout his career on the bench has worked with wide players such as Joaquín

---

266 Labarga, Nacho (2021). La Liga no longer has any dribbling: "There are no more Figos trying to take you on". *La Liga se queda sin regate: "Ya no quedan Figos que siempre intenten desbordarte"*. Marca

Sánchez, Arjen Robben and Jesús Navas, is also in the same vein: "With players like Luis Fabiano and Kanouté, who are good headers, Jesús Navas with his natural foot was perfect. If I had put a left-footed player on the right and a right-footed player on the left in that team, surely, they wouldn't have centred so many balls for them to finish. I think that if you have good strikers, the natural leg is essential and necessary"[267].

Bojan Krkić, a natural-born centre-forward, was deployed as a wide forward in Guardiola's Barça team in 2010. The change of Eto'o for Ibrahimović in the team that had just won a treble had not worked out as expected, and at the end of the season, with the team already eliminated from the Champions League and having to fight the league until the end against Manuel Pellegrini's Madrid, Pep made a decision: Lio Messi would once again finish the season as a false 9, in the same position from which he had subdued Real Madrid and Manchester United a year earlier. This time, however, the Argentinian's relocation did not shift the team's centre-forward to the wing, but rather ousted him from the eleven. Unlike Samuel Eto'o, who experienced his last days as a Barcelona player from the right wing, Ibrahimović was relegated to the bench. And Guardiola's bet to accompany Messi was the canteranos Pedro and Bojan, who completed the Barça attack in the difficult away games against Villarreal and Sevilla, and in the final and last game against Valladolid at the Camp Nou. Three games ended with three definitive victories, five goals from Messi, two from Pedro and two more from Bojan.

In the same way that Thierry Henry did before and David Villa did just after, the Catalan had to adapt his apprenticeship as a centre-forward to the role of winger: "It's not the same playing as a left winger in a team like Barça, with

---

267 *En un momento dado* (2021). Interview with Juande Ramos. Extracted from: https://eumd.es/2021/04/entrevista-juande-ramos/

the players they had and the idea of the coach they had, to playing in a team that has a striker like Kanouté, for example, and in which the winger has to go to the back line to cross. There are many types of wingers. The position I was in didn't ask me to go to the back line and cross with my left foot, but it gave me freedom of movement, with participation and a very attacking character"[268].

The evolution of the wingers distinguished two families. The first, a direct response to the volume of play acquired by the strikers away from the final goal, is defined by the runs from the flank towards the inside of the area to ensure their occupation. With it, teams seek to exploit the play of the strikers outside the box without giving up the threat of a player close to the opposing goalkeeper, so that the movements of the 9 approaching the midfield are combined with those of one of the wingers bursting into the box. "The good thing about playing with this striker profile is that you're not in a winger position the whole game and Leo is a false nine," says Bojan Krkić, "I like it when there's an interchange of positions and the defender doesn't always have the same striker as the striker. That gives the team a lot of dynamism and creates doubts for the opposition, because sometimes they have a player in front of them who can go deep, other times they have a player who asks more for the ball at the foot or who can combine".

Stars such as David Villa at Messi's Barça, Cristiano Ronaldo at Benzema's Madrid, Sadio Mané at Roberto Firmino's Liverpool or Heung-min Son at Harry Kane's Tottenham perfectly exemplify this typology of wide attackers and their link with the characteristics of a new class of centre-forwards.

A symbiotic relationship in which those who start from the flank with the desire to finish in the box find their des-

---

268 *En un momento dado* (2021). Interview with Bojan Krkić. Extracted from: **https://eumd.es/2021/04/entrevista-bojan-krkic/**

tiny liberated, and those who abandon it to participate in other areas of the field find an ally so that their adventure does not require them to pay a toll. It is no coincidence that many of the wingers employed in such roles have a history of playing up front, as regular guests in the home that they now conquer by surprise. Guardiola, who saw first-hand how Johan Cruyff adapted the Bulgarian Hristo Stoichkov to the task in a Barça team that played with Michael Laudrup as a false 9, emulated his master by accommodating players like Thierry Henry, David Villa and Gabriel Jesus on the wing. "Pep played Villa as a winger. He wasn't a winger, and he played a different role," recalled his assistant Domènec Torrent in an interview with El Periódico newspaper. "He opened up the field, and when playing with a false nine like Messi who came down, Villa would cut into the space between the full-back and the centre-back. We didn't give it to him at the foot because we wouldn't have taken advantage of it in the same way "[269]. A process of adaptation to the winger's area, after years installed in the penalty area, which in 2020 Villa recalled in the programme "Universo Valdano":

"At the beginning I was a bit scared. My fear wasn't so much that I wouldn't be able to adapt to the wing, but that my goalscoring figures would drop and that this would affect my performance. I lived from scoring goals. But then I realised that starting from that position I also had the freedom to reach the goal. I could even play a more important role than playing as a 9, because on the wing I received more balls. I remember a chat with Vicente del Bosque when he asked me if I'd prefer to go back to the centre. I told him: "Coach, I'm happy to play on the left.

Guardiola made me see other things about the game. Until then I had been a 9, and I had had minimal tactical demands. I was a finisher, and I didn't participate much in

---

269 Domènech, Joan (2019). Domènec Torrent: "With the 4-3-3 you can play anywhere in the world". *El Periódico de Catalunya.*

the construction of the game. And defensively I only had to be between centre-backs and go back to midfield a bit... I didn't have many tactical demands. But when I arrived in Barcelona and started playing on the left, I started to see other things. When the full-back would go up, when to come out and press, when to join up with the midfield, when to cover the full-back, when to go inside to get the full-back to go up... I learned a different way of playing football"[270].

Something similar had happened two seasons earlier to Thierry Henry when Guardiola chose the Frenchman for the same left winger role. He was the master of the position when Jeffrén Suárez first appeared in the first team and the mirror in which he would look to learn the needs of the position: "For me, Henry was the best winger in the world. Learning from him was a blessing. He once explained to me how I had to move into space. He told me to look at the body language of the player with the ball to see if he was going to pass into space or to the foot. And if the pass was going to go to the foot, I had to first pretend to go into space and then come back to receive at the foot. Because that way I received with space, without the defender on top of me, and I had time to think. When I wasn't playing, during the games I would watch him. Even today, when I play as a winger, I still have movements that I used to do back then".

As well as being particularly suited to the new uses of the centre-forward, the conversion of David Villa and Thierry Henry also gave the strikers space that they would not have found near the penalty area and against opponents who had dropped off. This is how Cruyff explained his decision to put Stoichkov on the wing, and his previous attempt to do the same with Englishman Gary Lineker: "Lineker, like Stoichkov, is a player with pace, but we were playing in the opposition half and there the space to the

---

270 *Universo Valdano* (2020). "David Villa". Movistar +

goal is tiny. So, if you have pace, you need more space to make the most of it. That's why they both played as wingers without being wingers"[271].

Similar cases have been those of France's Kylian Mbappé and Germany's Timo Werner, strikers who, despite knocking on the door of the elite in a central attacking position, have also been used by their coaches on the wing, taking advantage of their speed when it comes to diagonally cutting into the box.

If the first family of new wingers popularised a type of wide attacker who, starting from the edge of the box, maintained a close relationship with the penalty area and the finish, the second is a consequence of the cornering of the playmaker. Firstly, because they have provided a place from which to express themselves for those who could not fit into midfield duties. And secondly, because with the classic figure of the playmaker disappearing, the space in front of the midfield and immediately behind the striker was available for these players to occupy by coming to the centre from the edge. The flank as the new home of the 10.

There are few more emblematic examples of this than that of the Lio Messi when at Barcelona, a midfielder with a vocation, very protagonist with the ball, whom Frank Rijkaard introduced into the team's dynamic as an atypical right winger. The Argentinian, who as a promising teenager recognised his taste for receiving a lot of balls and "having them for a long time", the coach did not ask him to be a strict footballer holding onto the flank but gave him the edge as a less crowded space than the centre and in which, therefore, it would be easier for him to come into contact with the ball. "When I came into the first team, Rijkaard sent me to play on the right. It was a totally new position for me, but I got used to it little by little," the Argentine told DAZN. "Over time I got used to the position. I got used to it quickly because playing on the opposite foot made it easy

---

271 *Recorda Míster* (2009). "Johan Cruyff". Barça TV.

for me to come inside with my strong leg and have a view of the pitch in front of me"[272].

A comfortable area to receive the ball, to direct his left foot towards the box and the midfield, and from where he could draw a diagonal to which both Rijkaard, and later Guardiola and Luis Enrique, entrusted a large part of the success of their respective cycles.

Lio's case was just another chapter in a story that, without going any further, in the Spanish league was also written by Madrid's Zidane or Barcelona's Rivaldo, Riquelme and Ronaldinho. Some more reluctantly than others. Particularly illustrative is the latter's relocation to Rijkaard's Barça, because unlike his predecessors, his was not an exercise in subordination to the tactical rigidity of his coach, but an adaptation to increase the player's comfort and influence. As an anecdote, in fact, Ronaldinho's presentation in front of his fans, at the Joan Gamper friendly trophy with which FC Barcelona welcomes each new season, took place as an unexpected wide man, something far removed from what the club expected with his recruitment, as attested to by the statements of Txiki Begiristain, then technical secretary: "We are all clear that Ronaldinho is a player for the centre, but he is one of the alternatives available to the coach"[273].

However, Barça's poor start to the season prompted the club to reinforce their squad with the arrival of Dutchman Edgar Davids on loan, a seemingly temporary operation which, nevertheless, led to a tactical facelift that was key to the subsequent fortunes of the project. The arrival of the midfielder led Frank Rijkaard to alter the organisation of the team, until then a 1-4-2-3-1 with Xavi Hernandez in the double pivot and Ronaldinho in the midfield, to em-

---

272 Falcó, Álvaro (2020). *Tribuna*: Leo Messi explains how Frank Rijkaard made him a right winger. Extracted from: **https://tribuna.com/es/fcbarcelona/news/2020-01-16-leo-messi-explica-como-frank-rijkaard-le-convertio-en-extremo-derecho/**

273 Martínez, Roberto (2003). Txiki: "*Ronaldinho ha tenido problemas en la derecha*". - "Ronaldinho has had problems on right side of the pitch", - *Mundo Deportivo*.

brace a 1-4-3-3-3 that would move the Catalan forward and relocate the Brazilian star to the left flank.

With Ronaldinho on the wing, not only did he find the perfect position to receive the ball with fewer opponents around him and with his magical right foot open to a panoramic view of the attack, but he also laid the foundations for much of the team's play. Receiving Rafa Márquez's long pass from defence, enjoying the company of three midfielders when partnering up, relying on the depth of the left-back to get out wide and finding two perfect receivers for his passes in the other two forward positions. "He would tell me: you run and only the ball will come to you," recalled Samuel Eto'o, with whom the Gaúcho native formed one of the most dangerous partnerships of the era[274].

Eusebio Sacristán, assistant coach during Ronaldinho's time at Barcelona, analyses the Brazilian's adaptation to a wide position in the following terms: "During the period with Rijkaard we started to work on an attacking idea similar to the one we had had at Barça with Cruyff (...). We started to work the 4-3-3 with Ronaldinho on the wing to come inside and give us an extra man in midfield. Then we left Ronaldinho's flank for Gio or Silvinho to go up. On the other hand, our right-back was more like a third centre-back, because we had a more open winger like Giuly"[275].

Two different types of wingers. Initially, they were players with a wide angle, differentiated by the nature of their diagonal runs: one in the direction of the midfield and the other with the opponent's area as a target. Both destinations, however, with the centre of the attack as a common feature, a fact that is central to the popular use of wingers on the wing. Far from the old formulas that priori-

---

274 *Informe Robinson* (2009). "Samuel Eto'o". Canal +

275 *En un momento dado* (2021). Entrevista a Eusebio Sacristán. Recuperado de: https://eumd.es/2021/04/entrevista-eusebio-sacristan/

tised the right-footed player on the right and the left-footed player on the left so that their more natural dribbling position would facilitate a vertical advance parallel to the touchline. The new link between the position and the inside areas favoured the opposite recipe, so that, starting from the whitewash, a left-footed striker on the right and a right-footed striker on the left could orientate his more skilful leg towards the centre. Looking into the box and not towards the corner flag.

"Football changes every decade. It has nothing to do with the way it is played now compared to the way it was played in the 90s or later, when I was at Madrid," Savio Bortolini, a left winger who played on the left flank for Flamengo, Real Madrid and the Brazilian national team in the late 90s, told Marca newspaper. "The tactical side has changed and the number of skilful players who play one-on-one and cross for a goal has decreased. Now they play on the inside and with the inside out" [276].

Thus, the use and enjoyment of wingers, combined with the disappearance of midfielders and the mobility of strikers, has reaffirmed the consolidation of one of the most dominant figures of its time: that of the goalscoring wing forward. Footballers with the determination of true predators in the penalty area gifted with a tactical context that puts up no barriers to the conquest of their spoils.

Eusebio Sacristán is a coach who has very often used his wingers on the wing: "If you have wingers on the outside, with their natural legs, and all they do is dribble and cross, in a way they are limiting themselves. It's preferable to have them for finishing, to have them go inside so they can finish. You need people at the end, and you have people at the end with the striker but also with the wingers. You need your wingers to get into the box. The full-backs,

---

276 Labarga, Nacho (2021). La Liga no longer has any dribbling: "There are no more Figos trying to take you on". *La Liga se queda sin regate: "Ya no quedan Figos que siempre intenten desbordarte"*. *Marca*.

with natural legs, can be the men who put the cross into the box. Those are the ones who go out wide".

Along the same lines, Argentine coach Ariel Holan also expressed his opinion: "When you play with wingers on the wing, it's generally because coaches favour the natural movements that these players have to come inside and finish. Because at the same time they have full-backs who pass very deep. So they have two possibilities: either the winger hooks and shoots with the goal in front of him and dribbling over the opponent's weak leg, or the winger or a midfielder dribbles and overlaps out wide"[277].

"Pedro started playing on the outside, but when you saw Dani Alves start to come up the flank he would go inside. If he didn't receive the ball, he would go deep", adds Jeffrén Suárez on the relationship between the winger and the full-back in Guardiola's Barça.

In addition to the alternation that Lio Messi and Cristiano Ronaldo have maintained season after season as top scorers in European leagues, other examples, such as those of Sadio Mané and Mohamed Salah at Liverpool, Raheem Sterling at Manchester City, Heung-min Son at Tottenham, Kylian Mbappé and Kylian Mbappé at Manchester City are also examples, Kylian Mbappé and Neymar at PSG, Gareth Bale at Real Madrid, Arjen Robben and Franck Ribéry at Bayern Munich and even, in another register, cases such as Nicolas Pépé at Christophe Galtier's Lille or Lucas Ocampos at Julen Lopetegui's Sevilla, put names and surnames to the mould.

The recent popularity of advanced interiors, as well as the use of full-backs away from the flank and into the attack from more central areas, however, opens the door to the return of the classic wingers. Freeing up the midfield for the midfielders to move forward and widening the pitch as the only wide attackers. This is the opinion of Álvaro

---

277 Ariel Holan DT (15th September, 2015). Ariel Holan DT | *Escuela Técnica*. Extracted from: **https://youtu.be/VDT74nw-uq0**

Benito, for whom these modifications could also herald the return of wing attackers playing with their natural legs: "I think that the winger with his left foot is very useful for getting the ball. In the end, he is often just another playmaker who gets in behind the line. Today's football I think is moving towards the vertical, and that will bring back the natural winger. The dribbler"[278]. Players in charge of occupying the flanks, enlarging an interior space very crowded with team-mates and opponents, insistent in 1v1 situations and with the ability to feed the area in search of finishers.

---

278 *En un momento dado* (2021). Interview with Álvaro Benito. Extracted from: https://eumd.es/2021/04/entrevista-alvaro-benito/

CHAPTER 9

THE FALSE 9

> "A modern centre forward is not only about goals. I watch football, not just the goals"[279]
>
> KARIM BENZEMA

Real Madrid and FC Barcelona were playing at the Santiago Bernabéu in a match that would be crucial for the outcome of La Liga. The leaders of the league, the *Blaugranas*, were on course for what would eventually be the first treble in their history, but their draw at Valencia the previous day tightened their grip on the top of the standings. Pep Guardiola's side arrived at their arch-rivals' stadium four points clear, ahead of a trip to Stamford Bridge and a trip to Camp Nou to host Villarreal. Real Madrid, led by Juande Ramos, who made his debut as coach in the first clásico of the season, had enjoyed a string of very positive results in La Liga since the coach's arrival, with a record of 17 wins, interrupted only by a draw against Atlético de Madrid. Although the match was not going to

---

279 Polo, Pablo (2017). Benzema: "A modern centre forward is not only about goals. I watch football, not just the goals". *Marca*.

directly change the league standings, the feeling was that whoever won the game would eventually lift the title. "We knew that if we lost that game it would be very difficult," Guardiola would later say[280].

It was six minutes into the game when the Barça coach walked towards his technical area, raised his arm and signalled his attackers to change positions. Samuel Eto'o, until then the team's centre-forward, moved to the right, while Lio Messi, who had started the game lying on the wing, moved to the centre as a false nine. The rest, as they say, is history.

The Culés won 2-6 away at the home ground of their main pursuers, with a display of football that their opponents were unable to decipher and which helped them to seal the league title. It was a victory that began to build on Lio Messi's new position up front and the role that Guardiola brought back for the Argentine: the false 9. "It was a surprise for me," recalled Lio in 2020, interviewed by DAZN. "Guardiola told me that he had been watching a lot of Real Madrid matches, that he had been talking about it with Tito Vilanova and that they had thought he was going to play as a false 9. He was going to send Eto'o and Henry out wide, and I would be in the centre to link up with the midfield as well"[281].

Positioned in the centre of the attack and escorted by two wingers on the flanks, the Argentinian's position would be smoky, preventing any opposing player from being able to fix his defensive references on him. Behind the opposing pair of midfielders and in front of the two centre-backs, halfway between the four and too far away from all of them, his freedom was a permanent invitation to trap. If one of the centre-backs wanted to go out to

---

280 DjMaRiiO (2020, 5th February). Pep Guardiola and DjMaRiiO. Extracted from: https://youtu.be/RoEw-QkMP2A

281 Calemme, Mirko (2020). Messi: "My clashes with Cristiano Ronaldo will stay forever". As.

meet him, he was obliged to break the line and separate from his team-mates, leaving the full-back with no help and the other centre-back alone defending the box. That is how Henry's first goal that night came about, attacking the theoretical area of Fabio Cannavaro, the Real Madrid right centre-back whom Messi had lured into the centre of the pitch.

If, on the other hand, to avoid such a scenario, the onus fell on the midfield to defend Lio, one of the Whites' pivots would have to drop back and play deep, away from his midfield partner. As soon as this happened, Gago or Lass Diarra would play alone against Xavi, Iniesta and Yaya Toure. Apparently there was no antidote to the threat Guardiola had proposed. Messi, as a false 9, would be neither a striker nor a midfielder, but at the same time he would be both.

"It's a complicated position to defend," says Óscar García, Guardiola's Barça team-mate before they both embarked on coaching careers. "The false 9 can be playing up top, drop into midfield, drop to the wing... it's very difficult to mark. The centre-backs often don't know whether to go out or stay in. If they don't go out, the false 9 can receive alone, and that profile of player is usually skilful and has the ability to face you. But if they do come out, they leave the space between the centre-back and the full-back free for the winger to attack"[282].

The latter is also pointed out by Juande Ramos, Real Madrid's coach in that match, when he acknowledges that "surely, if the centre-backs had gone out to Messi's area, Henry or Eto'o would have entered those gaps left by them and it would have been even more dangerous for us"[283].

---

282 *En un momento dado* (2021). Interview with Óscar García. Extracted from: https://eumd.es/2021/04/entrevista-oscar-garcia/

283 *En un momento dado* (2021). Interview with Juande Ramos. Extracted from: https://eumd.es/2021/04/entrevista-juande-ramos/

Although nobody expected it at the Santiago Bernabéu, Guardiola's gamble was not new. He had presented it in society, almost without giving it any importance, several months earlier, when Barça visited Sporting Gijón on matchday three, still without a league win. That day, to make up for the slip-ups against Numancia and Racing Santander, Pep opted to field Lio, Eto'o and Iniesta up front, handing the Argentinian the central lane and moving Andrés and Samuel to the flanks. The three shared four of the six goals the blaugranas scored against Manuel Preciado's team and pointed to a path that the coach would not recover until later.

Catalan Gerard Autet was one of the Sporting de Gijón defenders who struggled with the novelty of the false nine. The centre-back, who was sent off for bringing down Lio Messi as the Argentinian was heading towards Sergio Sánchez's goal, acknowledged that at the time the false nine "was very new. It made you hesitate between going out or not going out. Up front your pivot had to take care of Barça's two inside players, and at the back there was Eto'o who could fix the centre-backs more... You thought: if I go out, I leave the defence very unprotected (...). That day Barça did a great job"[284].

After that game and until the Bernabéu, Barça spent most of the season with a more or less representative centre-forward, embodied in the figure of Samuel Eto'o. For Messi it would be the right wing, the one on which Rijkaard had given him a starting place in the first team, and where the 10 had played most of his minutes in the elite. Receiving on the left and ready to start a diagonal run towards the opposing goal, adorned with as many dribbles as the play required to finish in the opponent's box.

However, Messi's first season without Ronaldinho, the one of his first explosion as the team's standard-bearer,

---

284 *En un momento dado* (2021). Interview with Gerard Autet. Extracted from: https://eumd.es/2021/04/entrevista-gerard-autet/

had also proved to be a never-ending testing ground for his opponents. The Argentinian was already undoubtedly the centre of attention and the defensive obsession of anyone who came up against him. Consequently, attempts to stop him followed one after the other. Man-marking, aggressive marking, wing-backs to cover his lethal inside-out approach... The Argentinian managed to overcome them all, although there were two adjustments that added more discomfort to his game than the rest.

Given his dangerous runs with the ball from the wing, and his deadly touchdown on the edge of the box, some coaches first chose to focus more on defending the Argentinian's destinations than his runs. That is, to occupy the area of the pitch he wanted to reach, placing a midfielder to the left of the pivot, erecting a barrier at the end of the path that Messi repeatedly took from the flank. Secondly, another way of presenting himself to Lio consisted of direct confrontation against attacking full-backs. In this way, the opposing coach forced the Argentine to add kilometres of wear and tear to his legs, running backwards so as not to compromise the security of his defence.

The use of Messi as a false 9 shed light on both issues. Positioned from the start of the action in the central lane, his access to the edge of the area would be given in advance. He would not have to arrive; he would already be there. And furthermore, from the centre of the attack and with a team-mate on each side, the responsibility of following the opposing full-backs would be delegated. This is what Guardiola himself acknowledged to Ara journalist Antoni Bassas in an interview in 2019: "Beyond the offensive issue, I took Messi off the wing and put him in the middle for defensive reasons. The full-backs, in Europe, go forward a lot, and I didn't want LiOo to have the physical wear and tear of chasing them. We needed him to be fresh so that his talent could decide in the last twenty or

thirty metres"[285]. Messi would rest in the centre, between the lines, waiting to receive a ball in the heart of the opposing defensive structure to dynamite everything.

Football archaeology tends to place the first false 9 in history in 1953. In a match played at the legendary Wembley Stadium between the national teams of England and Hungary, and with Nándor Hidegkuti as the protagonist of the 6-3 final score[286]. The then MTK Budapest striker's significance in the Hungarian victory was marked not only by the three goals he managed to score, but also by a novel attacking performance that the opposing defence failed to decipher. "He was a fireman going to the wrong fire"[287].

In other cases, however, it is argued that the origin of the false 9 can be traced back to earlier times, to figures such as the Austrian Matthias Sindelar or the Argentinian Adolfo Pedernera [288].

Be that as it may, it was also a role with precursors in Barcelona. Frank Rijkaard offered it to Ronaldinho, just as Rinus Michels did with Cruyff in the 1970s[289] and César Luis Menotti did with Maradona in the 1980s. But if before Messi there had been a name linked to the role of false 9 at Barça, it was undoubtedly that of Michael Laudrup.

Rescued by Cruyff after six seasons in Italian football, the Dane arrived at the Camp Nou to fill the foreign place freed up by Gary Lineker's transfer to Tottenham Hotspur. The Englishman, who had made his career as a centre-forward, had not adapted to a system of play that had him

---

285 *Diari Ara* (5th July, 2019). The complete interview by Antoni Bassas with Pep Guardiola. Extracted from: https://youtu.be/D4yx1NHNX-8

286 Giner, Jorge (2020). *Panenka*: Hidegkuti: the origin of the false '9'. Extracted from: https://www.panenka.org/miradas/hidegkuti-el-origen-del-falso-9/

287 Perarnau, Martí (2012). *Perarnau Magazine*: The first false 9 in history. Extracted from: https://www.martiperarnau.com/el-primer-falso-9-de-la-historia-2/

288 Umoh, Anthony (2018). Sindelar, Hidegkuti and Cruyff and the amazing similarities. Extracted from: https://medium.com/speakingsports/sindelar-hidegkuti-and-cruyff-and-the-amazing-similarities-6c08b7d0dd3e

289 Roldán, Francisco Javier (2020). *Rinus Michels. "The Dutch school arrives at Barça". "Rinus Michels. La escuela holandesa llega al Barça"*. Editorial Libro Fútbol.

drifting to the wing. In the football that the coach wanted to implement at the Camp Nou, the centre-forward would hardly have any space, and that is why the Dutchman felt that Lineker's speed would be better utilised playing on the wing. "He is a good player, the problem is that we play differently. With our system he couldn't play at 100 per cent. Even the positions were different. And between changing everything or changing Lineker, I opted for the latter", said the coach to explain his departure.

Michael Laudrup, on the other hand, a born playmaker, was the perfect player to play in tight spaces, and to give the team the possibility of having an extra midfielder camouflaged as an attacking midfielder. Carles Rexach, Cruyff's assistant, explained how the talented Dane fitted into the team: "As Laudrup went down to get the ball, we often used him to give us superiority in midfield. We played five against four because the opposing centre-backs didn't have the courage to come out into midfield, otherwise they would leave their team with only three defenders wide open"[290].

"Cruyff explained it very easily - Laudrup recalled years later - he said: we play without 9 because all the centre-backs in world football are more comfortable if they have a striker in front of them to score. If they don't have anyone, they don't know what to do (...). And that's what happened in many games, especially at the beginning. The centre-backs were looking at the bench asking the coach what to do. Whether to come out and mark me or stay back, and as they didn't normally come out, we had one more player in midfield"[291].

Despite such illustrious precedents and the success with which Messi and Guardiola's Barça elevated their roles, the false 9 has not managed to be a particularly popular

---

290 *Recorda Míster* (2009). "Johan Cruyff". Barça TV.

291 TV3 (27th November, 2019). *Quan s'apaguen els llums*: Michael Laudrup. Extracted from: **https://youtu.be/pD-AzlwOUeU**

figure in the football that followed the successes of that team. It has not generated an extensive list of followers as, for example, the evolution of goalkeepers, centre-backs or the fortunes of the 1-4-3-3. If after Víctor Valdés, Dani Alves, Gerard Piqué, Sergio Busquets, Xavi Hernández and Andrés Iniesta there were many who, to a greater or lesser extent, tried to be like them, after Messi's false 9 only a very small group of brave players tried to emulate the Argentinian in this particular role.

Even Guardiola, the father of the creature, despite trying out Götze or Ribéry in Munich, and resorting to it in Manchester in the names of Phil Foden, Bernardo Silva or Kevin de Bruyne, after separating his path from that of Leo Messi, has prioritised attacking structures in which the clearest reference of a centre forward could be distinguished. One of the main reasons for this can be found in the colossal goalscoring figures of the Argentine footballer. A flair for goal that gave his team the virtue of combining the benefits of a false 9 with the goalscoring prowess of a typical penalty area predator. Messi was a false 9, apparently separated from the final goal but, in reality, equally linked to it.

"At Bayern —Martí Perarnau recalls— Guardiola found he didn't have the players to do it. Ribéry preferred to stay on the wing and, above all, he lacked goals. And a false 9 without a goal is not a false 9. Mario Götze couldn't be one either. (...) At City he has used it more often, but he usually does it against a very specific type of opponent. For example against Manchester United he does it almost always (...). The false 9 should not be institutionalised permanently. It's better to use it more tactically than strategically", concludes Martí[292].

In the same direction Bojan Krkić points out that "when the false 9 plays more alone, with two wide open wingers,

---

292 *En un momento dado* (2021). Interview with Martí Perarnau. Extracted from: https://eumd.es/2021/04/entrevista-marti-perarnau/

it's a system that needs to be very well worked so that the inside players can get there, or so that the wingers can give you depth, because otherwise it loses strength (...). If the false 9 is accompanied by two strikers placed between the centre-back and the full-back, he can link up with the midfield, having two references in front of him"[293].

Óscar García resorted to the figure of the false 9 as coach of the Barça youth team in which players such as Gerard Deulofeu and Rafinha Alcántara played. "We had problems playing with a more typical 9 because Mauro Icardi left, and we thought Rafinha was a player who could play this role perfectly. He was always well positioned to receive the ball, he had a lot of skill, and that season he was very inspired in front of goal and had a magnificent year", the coach analyses, although he does not overlook the complexity of this solution. "If you do not have players on the wing who can give you depth, you can dominate the game but you can't get forward. At that time in the youth team we had players like Ernesto, Deulofeu or Armand Ella, who could attack the space left by Rafinha very well. They were very quick players going into space and very good one-on-one (...). It's not easy to find a player who can play as a false 9. Who always has a good body orientation to receive the ball, who knows how to turn, who controls space and time, who is good one-on-one and who also scores goals. How many players like that can you find? There are very few".

This is something that Perarnau also agrees with, underlining that "throughout history, the role of false 9 has been reserved for the best players. The best players in history have been false 9s. Maybe not throughout their sporting careers, but at certain very important moments. Messi was a false 9, Maradona was a false 9, Cruyff was a false 9, as were Gerd Müller, Di Stéfano, Bobby Charlton, Ray-

---

293 *En un momento dado* (2021). Interview with Bojan Krkić. Extracted from: https://eumd.es/2021/04/entrevista-bojan-krkic/

mond Kopa, Nandor Hidegkuti or Matthias Sindelar. The list of false 9s is very similar to the list of the best players in history".

When you don't have a player of that dimension, therefore, the false 9 is a complex and demanding position that assumes, from its inception, the vacancy of the area of the pitch closest to the goal. It eliminates the reference that, ultimately, teams throw against opposing goalkeepers. The piece that often makes it possible to simplify the attacking play thanks to his mere presence. Johan Cruyff, architect of the false 9 played by Michael Laudrup in the "Dream Team", was along these lines when justifying the arrival of a centre forward like Romário in a team that in previous years had dispensed with this type of player: "He has the virtue that if balls arrive in the box he can score a goal. He transmits this calmness to the whole team, who can be sure that he will score. This is what we didn't have last season"[294].

It is not for nothing that the most satisfactory experiences in the use of the false 9 have taken place in three types of team. Firstly, in those, the most fortunate ones, that have enjoyed an executor with great goalscoring ability and whose relationship with the goal has not been affected. This is the case of Lio Messi's story at FC Barcelona, of Dušan Tadić at Ten Hag's cheeky Ajax, who in 2019 came within one goal of the Champions League final, or of Luciano Spalletti's Roma, who in 2006-2007 saw Francesco Totti lift the Golden Shoe as European football's top scorer[295].

Secondly, the false 9 has been successful in teams that were able to accompany him with goalscoring certainties in other positions. Generally on the flanks. For example,

---

294 Morén, Albert (2016). *En un momento dado*: Romário in the penalty area. Extracted from: https://eumd.es/2016/09/repaso-temporada-romario-barca-johan-cruyff/

295 Bordocampo (2012). *Roma di Spalletti*. AS Roma under Spalletti. Extracted from: https://bordocampo.wordpress.com/2012/02/11/analisi-la-roma-di-spalletti/

Mané and Salah in Roberto Firmino's Liverpool, or Cristiano Ronaldo in Karim Benzema's Madrid, those seasons in which both the Brazilian and the Frenchman have come closest to playing a false 9 role in their teams' attacks. "With Cristiano Ronaldo I changed my game," acknowledged Benzema in a conversation with Jorge Valdano. "I played for him. There was a player who scored twice or three times as many goals, and I had to adapt by giving more assists or making moves (...). A player can be capable of scoring 50 goals, but if the others don't get the ball to him or don't create space for him, he won't be able to score them", the Frenchman explained [296].

Finally, thirdly, the false 9 has also worked in teams capable of making the most of their goals, and for whom, therefore, reducing their ability to score goals did not mean they were far from victory. Along these lines, the Spanish national team won Euro 2012 by playing half the games (including the final against Italy) without a single natural striker, with Sergio Busquets, Xabi Alonso, David Silva, Xavi Hernández, Andrés Iniesta and Cesc Fàbregas in front of the defence. With the latter playing as a false 9, in a role that Del Bosque also used to eliminate Germany in the 2010 World Cup, with Pedro Rodríguez in the role of false offensive reference.

Although the false 9 has not become a mould with which to manufacture replicas that emulate a prototype linked to success, his figure does represent the most extreme aspect of a trend. Of a way of understanding the position and functions of the centre-forward that stands in opposition to the previously prevailing preferences. The confrontation between an older model of striker, intimately and sometimes exclusively linked to finishing, and a type of striker who, in modern times, will be asked to be more involved in the game in a broader and more multifaceted way.

---

296 *Universo Valdano* (2020). "Karim Benzema". Movistar +

On the threshold of the new millennium, few figures have enjoyed more popularity and standardisation than the 9-goaler. Players of diverse typologies but carved by the same shared destiny: the final gesture. Footballers who often took little part in phases of the game other than finishing, and in areas of the pitch other than the opposing penalty area. Men whose arsenal of attributes was oriented, almost entirely, towards the same end. Their positioning, their runs, their contact with the ball and their reading of the game were all aligned with the search for a goal. Experts in the penalty area, masters in the art of finishing and masters of a specific sensibility when it came to reading balls close to the opponent's goal.

During those years, the ball could cross the world by leaping from the head to the head of the specialist strikers in the penalty area. For example, the European Championships in 2000 in Belgium and the Netherlands, which featured a large number of nine strikers in its line-up. Virtually every participating team brought their own: Oliver Bierhoff, Ulf Kirsten and Carsten Jancker in Germany; Shearer, Heskey and Kevin Phillips in England; Pauleta in Portugal; Viorel Moldovan and Adrian Ilie in Romania; Filippo Inzaghi and Vincenzo Montella in Italy; Hakan Şükür in Turkey; Urzaiz in Spain; Tore André Flo in Norway; Savo Milošević, Darko Kovačević and Mateja Kežman in Serbia and Montenegro; Jon Dahl Tomasson and Ebbe Sand in Denmark; Trezeguet in France; and Van Nistelrooy, Makaay and Van Hooijdonk in the Netherlands. All of them filled a list of strikers that did not include other illustrious players such as Fernando Morientes, Jimmy Floyd Hasselbaink, Andy Cole, Andriy Shevchenko and Christian Vieri.

On the American continent, the factory was equally fertile, with names such as the Argentinians Batistuta, Crespo and Martín Palermo; the Mexicans Borgetti, Luis Hernández and Cuauhtémoc Blanco; the Chileans Salas and Zamorano; and the Brazilians Ronaldo, Giovanni Elber, Sonny Anderson and Mário Jardel, who took up the baton from such greats as Romário, Bebeto and Edmundo. Virtually every nation tied its flag to a striker of the same bloodline.

Some of them, however, lived between two eras, as in the case of Ronaldo Nazario or his compatriot Adriano Leite. They were footballers equally carved by the pattern of the shot, but whose ability to reach it enjoyed a self-sufficiency superior to that of their contemporaries. In a football that gradually ceased to be at the service of its strikers, and to be built on the paths that served as food for them, the 9s had to learn to hunt alone. Literally, too, because the proliferation of more conservative proposals in terms of sheltering their strikers was accompanied by the gradual forgetting of a recipe that had made a fortune in the past: the pairing of strikers.

Tandems of attackers, sometimes complementary and sometimes with much more shared characteristics, were broken up in favour of formulas that gave the centre of the attack to a single player. Often without a partner and often without care[297].

"I like to play with two strikers. It seems to me that when you play with just one striker, the area is a little under-supplied", admits Juande Ramos, manager for two seasons of a Sevilla team crowned by the partnership formed by Frédéric Kanouté and Luís Fabiano.

"A coach told me: whenever you take a team that is not a big team, put two strikers. Because you're always going to scrape something. A mistake, a two for two, a defender who slips, a long ball... anything. You're always going to have two players fluttering around," explains Álvaro Benito. If you're a team with the ability to dominate the game a lot and to play a lot in the opposition half and in the box,

---

297 Ustáriz, Eduardo. (2020). Football Hunting: The last big change of the centre forward. Extracted from: https://footballhunting.wordpress.com/2020/04/21/el-ulti-mo-gran-cambio-del-delantero-centro/

you can afford to play with just one striker, because in the end the wingers are going to end up playing a lot in the box, the midfielders are going to get there too and you can afford not to have so many people fixed in positions in the box"[298].

After the 2006 World Cup, an event in which more classic striker profiles such as Miroslav Klose, Hernán Crespo and Luca Toni still stood out, the top level, as far as the centre-forward position was concerned, was taken over by players capable of surviving on their own. Whether through technical brilliance, physical superiority or a combination of both, strikers such as Samuel Eto'o, Thierry Henry, Didier Drogba, Fernando Torres, Wayne Rooney, Robin van Persie or Zlatan Ibrahimović became the benchmark. Autonomous strikers whose teams needed them to be involved beyond the finishing line and the penalty spot. Strikers with the ability to carry a greater workload on their shoulders, responsible for activating many more metres with their play, and for taking on alone responsibilities that had previously been shared. The team no longer played for them.

Thus, little by little, we went from a football where teams put their game at the service of strikers who were eminently finishers, to another in which it was the strikers who would put themselves at the service of the game. They ceased to be spearheads and became just another piece of the collective gear. Just like the goalkeepers, the strikers also cut the shackles that held them to the goals to open up the horizon of their game and their place in the team.

For me it's an evolution of football," comments Óscar García, "now the pure centre-forward who shoots purely from the penalty area is practically only used in the second half when you're losing (...). It is difficult to see a winger

---

298 *En un momento dado* (2021). Interview with Álvaro Benito. Extracted from: https://eumd.es/2021/04/entrevista-alvaro-benito/

with natural legs. They use more wingers because they play more inside than outside, and with the disappearance of these natural wingers there are fewer crosses into the box and the 9-footer is disappearing. Another striker profile is being sought".

In this sense, the approach to more associative proposals in which control over the ball and the game has gained in importance, has shaped a type of striker who is especially adapted to his environment and oriented towards promoting the new objectives of his team. Away from their former role as finishing specialists, their colour palette has added shades and tools, multiplying the moments of the game in which they must participate and the ways in which they must do so. Versatile strikers, capable of combining close to midfield, of occupying the flank by providing relays for the wingers, of opening up space for the second line and of keeping active in defensive duties. All this without losing their atavistic relationship with the goal.

There are few more explicit statements about the number of roles that modern centre-forwards must embody in a single body than those made in 2016 by Luis Enrique, then coach of FC Barcelona. In a Barcelona side that was pulsating to the rhythm of the spectacular attacking trio of Messi, Neymar and Luis Suárez, the coach listed all the functions that the Blaugrana system of play demanded of its centre-forward as follows:

"At the start of the game he has to give us an outlet at times when the opposition presses us high, create space for us, lengthen the opposition defence, come and receive between the lines, play in front of us, get the ball into the box, when the ball is on the wing he can get to the near post or the far post depending on the situation, the opposition or depending on what we are most interested in... That's with the ball. Without the ball I also ask a lot of things of him. Fixing a centre-back and that if they defend with a line of three he knows how to wait for the ball to go to one of the sides to fix the centre-back and direct play where we want it to go, or that once the ball goes past him he comes to help the midfield line and press the opposing pivots. Just by focusing on that, that's enough for me. If he also scores goals, we'll all laugh"[299].

The modern centre-forward is required to have a permanent link with the game and a closer relationship with the ball, in functions and areas not always linked to the goal. Participating in the combination thanks to appearances in front of the midfielders, coming out of the box to allow the play to breathe. By offering, through his support on the front line, oxygen so that the ball's trajectories do not lose speed or intention. "Ibrahimovic is capable of giving mouth to mouth to a play; he makes dead moves breathe again"[300], Juanma Lillo illustrated when the Swede arrived at the Camp Nou to take the place of Samuel Eto'o, as a parenthesis prior to Guardiola's definitive bet on the false 9 Messi.

Zlatan, as well as being an aerial solution that would allow the central defenders to diversify their outlet by adding to their characteristic short passing game the presence of a receiver for a longer type of service, embodied the evolution of the demarcation within the Dutch school of play. That which had seen the disappearance of the figure of the 6, a pivot positioned between the striker and the midfield and whose play with his back to goal was essential for the midfielders to be able to receive the ball oriented towards the opponent's area.

"It was a position that allowed you to make the most of the arrivals from the second line, and which served to unload the play towards the midfielders who came in front of the goal. The option of the false 9 does a bit like that. To take advantage of the space behind the opposing mid-

---

299 Morén, Albert (2020). *En un momento dado*: After Luis Suárez. Extracted from: **https://eumd.es/2020/01/analisis-tactico-luis-suarez-barcelona-lesion-valverde-messi-xavi/**

300 Mundo Deportivo (2010). Lillo, number one supporter of Chygrynskiy and Ibrahimovic. *Mundo Deportivo*.

fielders to receive the ball there", analyses Óscar García. The youth academy player, trained in Barça's youth ranks as a midfielder, was one of the players to whom Johan Cruyff entrusted the role of 6, and would end up playing as a centre-forward during the coach's final period at Barcelona.

After the likes of Jose Mari Bakero and Jari Litmanen lost their place when the 1-3-4-3 dispensed with a midfielder to gain a fourth defender, part of his role fell to the centre forward. Attackers such as Oscar, Patrick Kluivert, Nwankwo Kanu and Dennis Bergkamp, or later Ibrahimović, who, while still inhabiting the 9's place, developed a greater sensitivity for association and, in particular, for playing with their backs to goal. He was the new resting point on which his team-mates could lean to get the ball back to their feet in the best possible conditions. "We were also finishers, but different from strikers like Romário or Ronaldo at that time. We didn't have as many resources as they did for individual play, but perhaps we were more associative and could combine outside the box," the Catalan points out.

Since 2008, as the importance of controlled ball control from the defence has increased, so has the willingness to press and reduce space when opponents try to start the play from the back. That's why, adds Bojan Krkić, "playing out from the back is very important (...), if you talk to defenders they will tell you that when it comes to bringing the ball out they really appreciate it when their team has a striker who can hold the ball up and give them pace (...). More than a height issue, I would say it has more to do with physical strength. Or with the type of play, because if you're used to that, you grow with that quality. I remember Giuseppe Rossi, who played for Villarreal and was probably shorter than me, but he was a beast at holding the ball back. He had a great quality protecting it from the defender and directing the ball".

In this way, the centre-forward's presence at the back of the pressure provides his team with a passing option, as a stepping stone for the ball to reach another teammate, or to turn on its axis and make a run towards goal. "Cruyff used to say to me: when you have the ball, the first thing you have to do is look to whoever is furthest away. The deepest. Romário, Laudrup... the deep one", explained Guardiola at a clinic held in Catalonia in 2007, before starting his career on the bench[301].

Strikers who are capable of playing with their backs to the box but facing the game, following the same pattern as Benzema, Roberto Firmino, Luis Suárez, Ibrahimović, Lautaro Martínez, Lukaku, Lewandowski, Agüero, Harry Kane and Duván Zapata. The Argentinian Juan Antonio Pizzi, who in the 1990s perfectly represented the prototype of the finishing centre-forward in the shirts of teams such as Rosario Central, Tenerife, Barcelona and River Plate, now coaches a very different profile of striker to that of that time: "There has been a radical change in the 9, with more complete, skilful players, with the qualities to associate and participate in the footballing circuit, whether it be in finishing or in the production of the ball. I think that has also been seen in England, which has been characterised by having big, strong strikers with good aerial play, where they are now looking for a bit more dynamics and association. It's one of the evolutions that football has undergone and that, for me, has strengthened the teams"[302].

The height at which opponents tend to position their defensive line, away from their own goal to join the rest of the team in pressing, is also a conditioning factor in the centre-forward's trade, as it pushes his actions far away from the opposing goal. Until the teammates at the back manage to overcome their opponents' harassment and

---

301 Arroyo, Natalia (2011). *El futbol, segons Guardiola. Ara.*

302 Marca (2020). Pizzi: "The biotype Lautaro Martínez has is the most suitable to adapt to Barcelona". *Marca.*

bring the game into the opponent's half, the game is more closely confined to their goalkeeper's domain than to the opponent's. The striker's offensive involvement, therefore, often starts from positions close to the halfway line.

"Often, the striker who is more of a finisher is a strong, big and not very fast type of player. That's why it hurts them when the opponent goes to press high and push forward the defensive line, because they are not quick attackers to go into space. It is more difficult for them to exploit their greatest strength, which is inside the box. That's why teams are now opting for fast strikers who can get out of the box well. That way they can take advantage of the spaces left by their opponents when they press high up the pitch," explains Óscar García.

The striker's ability to look for a deep, vertical run into space not only generates a personal benefit in the form of a goal, but also a more comfortable playing environment for the team. This is underlined by Bojan Krkić, pointing out that "the striker has to give the game this alternative to make the team long and push the opposition back", or Sergi Samper, from the midfield position, pointing out that "I especially like strikers who don't stop cutting into space. Because their runs give me a lot of solutions. If you can give them the ball, it's a goalscoring opportunity, but even if you can't give them the ball, they generate an infinite number of passing lanes inside. They are very important for the team"[303].

"If your two wingers go inside and the centre-forward goes down, in the end you are occupying the same position with three. It's very important that every space is occupied," reinforces another midfielder, Sergio Canales. For my game," continues the Cantabrian, "it's very important that the three up front have different characteristics. That is to say, if the left winger is a very vertical and unmarked

---

303 *En un momento dado* (2021). Interview with Sergi Samper. Extracted from: https://eumd.es/2021/04/entrevista-sergi-samper/

player, it's better for me if the centre-forward is the one who comes forward. The one who gives me the support and gives me an outlet to break the rival midfield line, or even to return the ball to me face to face. But on the other hand, if you have wingers on the other foot, with more of a tendency to cut inside or play one on one, I prefer a thousand times the centre forward to get out wide and look for depth"[304].

Ander Herrera insists on the same idea when he maintains that "success is in the mix. It wouldn't make sense for the two wingers to come looking for it and the striker as well. In the end you create an unnecessary funnel in midfield. One of the things I learned under Marcelo Bielsa is that there always has to be one or two players running into space to stretch the opposition. For example, at Manchester United we had Ibrahimović who loved to come and combine with the midfielders, but on the flanks we had Rashford, Lingard or Martial who were very good in space. And at Athletic Bilbao, although he played as a midfielder, one of the players who saw the space and the moment to run was Oscar De Marcos"[305].

For strikers, however, playing away from goal and against very advanced opposition defences also means having a lot of space in front of them. Enjoying a different scenario to that found by strikers of another era. For them, receiving the ball near the dividing line meant, almost inevitably, facing a backdrop that filled the space between them and the goal with a multitude of opposing players. Now, however, even if the strikers see the net from far away, they see it clearly and with few obstacles in the way.

Óscar García believes that this is the main reason why, despite the fact that strikers have gained more power and

---

304 *En un momento dado* (2021). Interview with Sergio Canales. Extracted from: https://eumd.es/2021/04/entrevista-sergio-canales/

305 *En un momento dado* (2021). Interview with Ander Herrera. Extracted from: https://eumd.es/2021/04/entrevista-ander-herrera/

their football has sometimes moved away from the penalty area, not only have their scoring figures not suffered but, in many cases, they have increased. The modern striker is not as tied to the finishing touch as his predecessors, but his link with the goal has remained. "When I played for Barça I knew I would attack in short spaces, but football is changing because opponents now press higher up the pitch. When you press higher up, if you don't recover on the first or second pressing and the opposition can overtake you, logically you will suffer defensively. It's not like being all eleven defending in your own half (...). It's also clear that when you press high you can steal balls closer to the opponent's area, being closer to the goal".

Bojan Krkić, for his part, introduces a second variable, in this case related to the protection of referees and the toughness of defenders. Being a centre-forward after 2010, concludes the Catalan, is no more difficult than before, even if it means having to play in more registers than in the past: "I think that if you talk to the players who played years ago, they will tell you that it wasn't easy to be a striker. Because of the type of defenders there were. They were tougher. Now football is also very physical, but surely defenders used to have a point of aggressiveness that they don't have now. Now I see defenders who stand out more for their quality and not so much for being that typical player who hit. Now defenders, even if they know how to defend well and are forceful, are finer (...). It wasn't easy to be a striker before, and it isn't easy now. Scoring goals is not easy".

The penultimate chapter in the evolution of centre-forwards, the penultimate stop on their journey, also hides a nod to their past. The dominance of strikers like Robert Lewandowski, Erling Haaland or even, despite their penchant for popping up outside the box, Romelu Lukaku or Zlatan Ibrahimović is reconciled with the tradition of expert finishers of yesteryear. With goal specialists. The growing impact of inside players near the box taking over areas that used to fall to strikers, the need for wingers to drop deeper to open up space for the midfielders, and the possibility of supplying the box from the flank thanks to crosses from wingers or full-backs, outline a new panorama with a multitude of alternative ways for the striker to create a dangerous chance, one that is generous when it comes to getting the ball to the striker without obstacles towards goal.

A fertile arsenal of solutions that does not always require prior involvement of the striker, and which requires a more specific figure to finish everything the team gives him. One final touch.

BIBLIOGRAPHY

ABOUT THE AUTHOR

Albert Morén (@eumd) was born in the city of Barcelona in 1986. In 2006 he created the football blog 'En un momento dado' (www.eumd.es), a space dedicated to tactical analysis especially linked to FC Barcelona current affairs. After covering Pep Guardiola's time at FC Barcelona between 2008 and 2012, he has followed the Catalan coach's progress at Bayern Munich and Manchester City. He has collaborated with projects such as Ecos del Balón, the magazines Panenka and The Tactical Room, and the programme Play Fútbol on Cadena SER, among other media.